THE U.S. CHILD SUPPORT SYSTEM AND THE BLACK FAMILY

How the System Destroys Black Families, Criminalizes Black Men, and Sets Black Children Up for Failure

Demico Boothe

Full Surface Publishing

Copyright © 2018 by Full Surface Publishing

All rights reserved. No part of this publication may be reproduced, distributed or transmitted in any form or by any means, including photocopying, recording, or other electronic or mechanical methods, without the prior written permission of the publisher, except in the case of brief quotations embodied in critical reviews and certain other noncommercial uses permitted by copyright law. For permission requests, write to the publisher at the address below.

Full Surface Publishing
P.O. Box 342405
Memphis, TN 38184
www.FullSurfacePublishing.com

Special discounts are available on quantity purchases by corporations, associations, and others.
For details, contact us at the address above.

1st ed.
ISBN 978-0-9792953-6-2
Library of Congress Control Number: 2017918455

"BREVITY IS THE SOUL OF WIT"

And for the sake of brevity, this reader has been made to be short and to the point. Also, the author fully understands that there is a child support system for each state within the United States, separate from each other but all governed in part by federal law, but will singularly use the term "child support system" within this text to give general reference to commonalities within them all or within the majority of them. Hence referencing them as one system.

Other books by Demico Boothe

Why Are So Many Black Men in Prison?

***Getting Out & Staying Out:
A Black Man's Guide to Success After Prison***

Chapters

Chapter One:
My Story p.1

Chapter Two:
A Summary on
When, Why, & How U.S. Child Support Laws Were Created p.37

Chapter Three:
Child Support and The Black Family:
What We Need from The System vs. What We Get p.47

Chapter Four:
A Flawed System That Sets Black Children Up for Failure:
Payments vs. Parentage, Dollar vs. Dad p.63

Chapter Five:
Another Form of Probation, Parole, & Control for Black Men:
Why Punitive Child Support Enforcement Procedures & Penalties
Tend to Affect Black Fathers Differently & Disproportionately p.85

Chapter Six:
Beware of "The Systems" p.110

Notation Sources p.122

All black people should pause for a minute and
ask themselves this question:
Where does my "education" come from?
If your education is not self-directed
or directed by those
who truly have your best interest at heart
and are properly informed about the past
as well as present-day reality,
and are truthtellers,
then you are not being educated;
you are being purposefully MISeducated
and TRAINED to serve those
who are, in fact, educated
because being truly educated
is about being made aware of the truth.

– Demico Boothe

CHAPTER ONE

My Story

"There are many truths of which the full meaning cannot be realized until personal experience has brought it home."
— John Stuart Mill, philosopher[1]

"You don't want the decisions about your children's lives to be in my hands or any other judge's hands. We don't know your kids, we don't understand your kids. You're five minutes on my docket. We're going to make the best decision we can, but we don't love them."
— Judge Lynn Toler, from the Divorce Court TV show[2]

    In 1992, at the age of nineteen and just months after graduating high school, I was convicted of possessing and selling a small amount of crack cocaine and sentenced to ten years in federal prison. This was my first time ever being in any kind of trouble with the law. At the time, I had only been selling drugs for a few months and was still living with my father. I did not even own a car. I went on to serve the entire ten-year sentence, minus one year for "good time," and was released at the age of twenty-eight. Sixty days after being released, I was back in federal prison on new charges. This time I wasn't guilty of what

I was being accused of, which was "attempting to purchase two hundred and fifty thousand dollars of counterfeit money in exchange for thirty thousand dollars in real money." (After serving all that time in prison and only being free for two months, I did not have even three hundred dollars to my name at the time, and certainly not thirty thousand.) It's a long story how this all happened to me just sixty days after being released, so to make a long story short, I took it to trial and fought it teeth and nails but was still convicted (the Feds have nearly a one hundred percent conviction rate,[3] so no surprise there). If you want more insight on this specific part of my life story, you will have to read my book, *Why Are So Many Black Men in Prison?*—the whole story about all that stuff is detailed inside there, but what is not in that book is the story about how I fathered a child, my first one, during those sixty days that I was a "free" man. My beautiful and beloved daughter, Oryanna Elizabeth Davis (Elizabeth is my mother's first name) was born on November 11, 2001 while I was serving yet another sentence of three and a half years inside federal prison for something I didn't do and *could not have done*, even if I had wanted to. And the judge, prosecutor, my probation officer, and the arresting Secret Service officers all knew it.

Oryanna's mother and I had been in a relationship for nearly five years before I came home from prison but we had known each other practically our entire lives. We had grown up together as teens on the same block, gone to junior high and high school together. We both knew each other's whole family. When I first went in to prison, we were only childhood friends. At around the halfway mark of my ten-year term, we became reacquainted and began conversing on the phone daily and she started regularly coming to visit me at the prison. This continued from that point until my release. Once I was released, Oryanna's mother and I planned to get married. In the beginning of our relationship, she had made me promise her that I would marry her if she faithfully stuck by me for the years I had left to do at that time, and I intended to fulfill my promise. She and my mother picked me up from prison on my release date and we immediately began living together at her apartment. Once we found out that she was pregnant, we expedited the wedding plans because she did not want to get married after the baby came; she wanted to do it before the baby came. While out shopping for a wedding dress with friends and family, she got the devastating phone call that I was back in prison.

At the time, because I had just been released from serving nearly ten years in prison sixty days earlier and was on probation and now had a brand new federal charge, everyone, including myself, automatically thought that I would be looking at serving a lot more time behind bars than I was actually facing. However, this new charge was considered "white collar crime" and carried much less time, unlike the crack cocaine charge I previously had. So, because she thought I would be gone again for possibly another ten years or more, from the day of my arrest my daughter's mother let it be known she wanted nothing more to do with me, and that our child was now *her* child; she literally said those words to me when I talked to her for the first time from jail after that incident occurred. Then, she completely cut me off over the next seven months while I went through my court and trial situation. She basically changed from my fiancé to a stranger, overnight. She would not accept any phone calls, would not assist me in any way, would not come to any of my court dates. Mind you, at this time, since I was actually innocent of the charges and was taking it to trial and not pleading guilty, it was not even a sure thing that I would be found guilty of anything. Plus, we eventually had come to find out that I was only facing a three-and-a-half-year sentence maximum, not ten years or more like everyone had initially thought. But because she had cut me off and was seemingly no longer concerned with my wellbeing and we were not communicating, once I was convicted she did not learn the actual time I had been sentenced to until I was almost finished serving the time. I ended up serving nearly three more years in prison for that bogus charge and conviction, then was released in 2004.

When my daughter was born, her mother and I had not spoken for seven months but my mother was with her in the delivery room and had been showing her emotional and financial support during the entire pregnancy, in my stead. My mother went to hospital visits and bought baby clothes and shoes. My mother spent several thousand dollars on a really nice extendable full bedroom set for my daughter before she was born, one that would last well into her teen years. While I was doing my time, my daughter's picture was the only picture on my cell walls. I was very grateful that my mom was there to help and that my daughter's mother was not financially dependent on me and would have no problem providing for our child in my absence. Still, I wanted so badly to get out and help raise her and support her so I began trying to prepare myself to be able to do so while I was still incarcerated. There were two main things that I did, while still incarcerated, that would go on to help me initially stabilize and maintain myself on the outside—I actually wrote and completed my first book, the aforementioned *Why Are So Many Black Men in Prison?* while serving that sentence, and I found a wife, who was an employee at the last prison I served time in that I got released from. So, once I got out my plan was to be an author, among other things, and get published and continue to write books about important issues that mattered to me and my community, and get married and start a family. I knew that it wouldn't be easy, and it wasn't, but it was what I eagerly looked forward to doing once I was released from prison for the second time.

  Upon my first release from prison in 2000, I had been immediately confronted with more issues and problems than I had ever imagined possible and I was totally unprepared to contend with all the tangible and intangible hardships that came my way. That time, I had gotten out of prison looking to just get a job and have a family, like any other citizen, and learned very fast that I was not like "any other citizen" and that there were gigantic obstacles in my way, especially with respect to getting a job. This second time though, I was getting out looking to be an entrepreneur and have a family; I had learned firsthand from my first release from prison that living-wage-paying jobs and black ex-felons don't go together in America. (I specifically say *black* ex-felons because studies have shown that white male ex-felons oftentimes have better paying job prospects and offers than blacks males with clean records or even college degrees.[4]) That second time around, I did everything I could think of to do to prepare myself to achieve my goals before I was even released, which I hadn't really done during that first sentence. I read hundreds of books and took every class I could that was offered in the prison. And it just happens that, while going through a nine-month early release prison drug program that was run by the psychology department of the Federal Bureau of Prisons, I met the woman who would later quit her job in the psychology department at the prison one week after I was released, move to Memphis where I was, become my wife and have my second child.

Two months before I was to be released, I received an unexpected letter from my daughter's mother. I had not heard from her in over two and a half years. In that letter, she described how she still loved me and had been missing me and had heard I was getting ready to get out and wanted to rekindle our relationship once I was released. I was shocked, to say the least. The handwritten letter was probably fifteen pages long. She said that she would be coming to visit me before I was released and asked me to call her immediately. I called her, and when she answered I asked her what was going on and why she had written such things to me after all that time. She stated that she wanted our relationship back and that she was sorry for ever abandoning me. She told me that she had bought a big house, for us, and wanted me to live there with her and our child when I came home. She said that she was not taking no for an answer and would be at the prison next week to see me. I informed her that she could not visit me because she was not on my visiting list at the prison, to which she responded, "I'm coming anyway, and I'm bringing the baby." After unsuccessfully trying to convince her not to drive all the way from Memphis to West Virginia in the middle of a snowy winter with our daughter in tow, I asked to speak to her mother, who was in the room with her at the time. Her mom got on the phone and told me that there was no convincing her not to come and that she was packing for the trip as we spoke. My daughter's mother got back on the phone and stated that it did not matter to her that she would not be able to see me;

she just wanted to prove her "love" for me by doing this and she was coming and that was all there was to it. I hung the phone up, not really believing that she would do such a thing. But she actually did come, with my daughter in tow as promised, and when the prison staff refused to allow her to visit me she just took a picture of herself outside of the prison, in the snow, with our two-year-old daughter, mailed it to me from the local post office, then drove home. The next time I spoke with her, I was a free man.

When I got released, prison guards dropped me off at the bus stop in Beckley, which is the small town in West Virginia where the prison is located. My future wife had taken off from work that day and was there waiting on me. When the guards left, she picked me up from the bus stop, and after spending a few hours at her home, she drove me to Memphis where we met up with my family for a brief time, then I turned myself in to the halfway house, where I had to serve six months. I had to physically live in the halfway house for two months before being allowed to live at home on "home confinement" for the remaining four months. (Halfway houses are for-profit businesses; while in the halfway house, inmates are required to get a job within two weeks of arrival and give the halfway house twenty-five percent of their gross monthly income "for room and board" or get sent back to prison. This fee still applies even when the inmates get put on home confinement.) Many inmates get sent back to prison from halfway houses because of job issues or income issues, but I was lucky enough to have a supportive mother and fiancé. During this transitional time, my fiancé moved to Memphis, found us an apartment, found another job, and immediately started planning our wedding. My mother owned a small cleaning business and she initially "hired" me when I first got there and paid me with company checks so that I could pay the halfway house fee (and basically guarantee that I would not get sent back to prison after two weeks for not being able to find a job) until I got myself together and started earning my own money.

  While I was in the halfway house, my daughter's mother gave me full access to our child. I could get her or go see her whenever I wanted. Had free reign with her. When I would go to see her though, her mother would have hot meals already prepared waiting on me when I got there, and sometimes had gift-wrapped presents for me along with it. Mind you, I had given her no reason to think that we ever would be together again, but I knew that she was doing these things to persuade me to be with her. I knew better than to encourage her, and I knew better than to discourage her too, if I wanted continued access to my daughter. I could sense that. So I did not discuss my personal business with her and had refrained from telling her about my new relationship and upcoming marriage because, as far as I was concerned, it was none of her business. Plus, I could certainly sense that she would probably not react well to that news.

Once I was released from the halfway house and allowed to stay at home for the remaining four months left on my sentence, my fiancé and I got married on her birthday, which was only a few days later. One of my cousins operated a small limousine service at the time, and his wedding gift for us was a free all-night limo cruise all around town. My cousin knew my daughter's mother, so I specifically had asked him not to mention my marriage to her or anyone that might tell her. He promised me he wouldn't tell anyone but I later found out that, just days after the wedding, he'd told several people from my old neighborhood. Of course, it got back to my daughter's mother and about three weeks after my wedding, just as I suspected would happen, I was cut off from my child again, but this time was also summoned to take a court-ordered blood test and appear in family court for a hearing. All I could think about was the fact that, besides this being totally unnecessary, I may have to face yet another hostile judge with power over my life, this time with it being given to him or her by my own daughter's mother, who undoubtedly would seek to harm me in whatever ways that could be justified and without regard to how that harm would or could affect our child's wellbeing and future. I dreaded having to be in yet another courtroom as a "defendant" at the mercy of the court, but I went.

In the courtroom, my daughter's mother did not speak to me or even acknowledge my presence. She was there, along with her mother. My daughter was nowhere to be found. Why her mother was there and not our daughter, I don't know. When given the chance to speak, I explained to the judge that I had just spent twelve years in prison and had just been released and did not currently have a job or stable income but stated that I was the father and bore responsibility to help take care of her. I explained the circumstances of my daughter's conception and the history of my relationship with her mother. When given the chance to talk, my daughter's mother spoke as if she was a victim of mine and asked for five hundred dollars a month. When the judge asked if she would like to receive back pay for the time I was in prison, she said yes. The judge chastised both of us for even having a child under such circumstances, and granted her back pay of nearly eight thousand dollars and, because I was "minimally" employed at the time, ordered me to begin paying two hundred and ninety-five dollars per month effective immediately. The judge also ordered that I have visitation rights and that our daughter's last name was now to be changed to mine. Now, barely one month after being released from physical custody after serving well over a decade in prison, I was virtually unemployed but with a debt of nearly eight thousand dollars hanging over my head and monthly financial obligations of two hundred and ninety-five dollars a month, plus the halfway house's twenty-five percent of my gross "income" for the next three months, in addition to normal household costs and living expenses.

Again, because of the much-needed support I initially received from my mother and my wife, I was able to keep up with my payments—for the first two years. While I had been in the halfway house, instead of focusing on finding a low-paying menial labor or fast food job like most inmates in halfway houses do, I had decided to start a sole proprietorship business—a commercial janitorial business, like my mother owned. So the first few weeks at the halfway house, when I was supposed to be out looking for work or "at work" at my mother's company, I was actually out soliciting contracts for my business; this was me and my mother's plan for me from the very beginning. And it paid off. After several weeks of walking business districts and handing out flyers and cold-calling, I was able to garner a few small contracts with several local companies to provide janitorial services for their office buildings. I didn't make much money because, in order to have my best chance at landing some contracts fast, I had to severely underbid other janitorial contractors, but I made enough to get off of my mother's payroll and start paying some of the household bills and my child support and halfway house fee myself. Plus, because I only actually worked about four to six hours a day on average, I often had enough extra time left in the allotted hours of the workday to work on getting my book manuscript ready for publication. I didn't have a computer or a printer of my own at the time, but I was able to use the one my wife had brought with her. I could not yet afford a car, but my mother let me utilize her car whenever I needed to. I worked my contracts and worked fervently on finalizing the book, while also trying to get more contracts so that I could make more money, but at a certain point I realized that it was too volatile a business type for me. My luck with the cleaning business seemed to haphazardly go up and down most of the time. I would get a contract, lose a contract. Get two small ones, lose one big one. And there were many contracts that I simply could not even go after because I lacked the equipment and manpower that it would take to do the job, or because they did background checks on their janitors. And I didn't want to always be borrowing my mother's few pieces of equipment, and renting the stuff was far too expensive. So, once I saw how hard it was to try and quickly grow that business with no significant resources or startup money, I began putting more energy and time into my book's editing and marketing and publication.

So that's basically how my first couple of years of freedom were spent—working and hustling hard trying to secure an immediate familial and short-term financial foothold in my life via smartly executed entrepreneurial ventures instead of a job. I had known that attempting this would be an uphill battle for a twice-incarcerated ex-prisoner like me, but again, despite me knowing that and doing all I could do to prepare for it, I was still ill-equipped to rightly handle so many obligations and get over so many hard obstacles so soon, and eventually did become overwhelmed. For two years, I had unsuccessfully tried to get my book picked up by a large publisher, to no avail. At the time, no one seemed interested in a book about a subject such as *Why Are So Many Black Men in Prison?*, penned by a black ex-convict who had just been released, and no such book had ever been published before. After soliciting nearly one hundred publishers with no success, I decided that I needed to start my own publishing company, the same way I had started the cleaning company, and publish my own book(s). I began to invest what little money I could glean every month into creating the company; obtaining publication equipment and software, finding editorial services and cover art design services, and doing a little pre-publication marketing and advertisement. I did all of this because I really believed I had a necessary and potentially bestselling exposé on my hands (which it did eventually become) and I figured if I got the book out within a year's time, things would then start to look up for me and mine in terms of stability.

Around the same time, I lost my main and best janitorial contract, the one that paid most of my share of the household expenses. I lost it because a newly hired black general manager wanted to replace me with a larger "more established and accredited" (his words not mine) white-owned company that charged much more money than I charged for the same services rendered. I didn't have a storefront for my business or the ever-so-popular monogrammed automobile and uniform with a company insignia on it, so I guess he figured I wasn't professional-looking enough to continue cleaning up their company's bathrooms and offices, which I had been doing for nearly a year with absolutely no complaints ever being made about me or my work. After the loss of that contract, I was spending more time at home working on my book and sending out emails and doing research for other book titles I wanted to eventually publish. I wasn't bringing home much money at all at this point. This is when I first started getting behind on my child support payments for my daughter, but I knew that if my plan worked and I got my publishing company off the ground, that everything would soon be okay. Then my wife told me that she was pregnant.

  My wife was not only a former psychologist for the federal prison system, she was also a Major in the Army, so once she moved to Memphis she immediately procured a part-time civilian position on the military base in Arkansas. When I lost my main cleaning contract and we found out she was pregnant, she applied for a full-time officer's position at the base but none were available for her rank at first. Which meant that, in the months leading up to our child's birth, we had to rely heavily on her part-time pay and her savings in order to make ends meet. During this time, even though I was doing all I could to get more contracts and get the book published, I certainly was not feeling good at all about having to rely on my pregnant wife's savings and income. Towards the end of the pregnancy she was offered the full-time position. My wife had two pre-teen kids from a previous marriage, so while she had been making the two-hour drives back and forth to Arkansas three times a week going to and coming from work, I was taking care of the kids; dropping them off and picking them up from school, making breakfast and dinner, helping with homework, all that. After our son was born, my wife resumed her job at the base. I continued to take care of the now three kids and do my cleaning thing and work on the publishing company and on my book, though it became much harder now that I had a newborn in the mix that didn't leave everyday like the other two kids did to go to school. During this time, it almost felt like I was a single parent because it seemed like my wife was never there. She would be gone before the kids got up for school each morning and would get back in around 6:30 in the evening, eat dinner and go to bed and do it all again the next day. Some days she would just spend the night on the base and not come home at all because she didn't feel like driving two hours in rush hour evening traffic back to Memphis.

After a few months of this, I started noticing that my wife seemed to be becoming stressed and withdrawn. So much so, that we consulted a doctor, who did eventually diagnose my wife with Postpartum Depression and recommend some marital counseling for us. We did go to counseling but it didn't solve anything. Not long after the counseling ended, my wife started avoiding me altogether. One Saturday morning, she awoke very early and left the bedroom and didn't come back for a few hours, but I didn't hear her making any movements and didn't hear her in the living room so I got up and looked for her and found her kneeling against the bed in her daughter's room. I got down on my knees next to her and asked what was wrong. She replied, "I just feel like the whole world is on my shoulders." I asked her what she meant by that and she didn't reply or explain. I remember promising her things would be better soon; that this was just the beginning of our lives together, but she didn't seem to be hearing that. For the next two weeks, my wife came home on Friday and got the kids and drove back to Arkansas where she spent the weekends on the base. That second weekend, when they got back home that Sunday night, her son came bounding through the door and cheerfully announced to me, "I saw our house in Arkansas and we're moving!" I was stunned beyond words.

I looked at my wife and asked if it was true. She said yes, it was true. I asked her why she was doing this. She then went on to explain that she now believes she just got caught up in the romance and adventure of our forbidden relationship and that life with me was not what she had expected it to be and that she felt she had made a mistake by marrying me. She really didn't have to say exactly why she felt that way because we both already knew why: I was broke with no clear future. She said that she had not previously understood how much of a struggle it would be for me once I got out of prison, but that she now realizes that she doesn't want that life for herself and her children. She told me that she indeed had been house shopping while in Arkansas for the past two weekends and had already cancelled our apartment lease and that we were expected to be out of our apartment within one week. She had done all of this, in secret. As time would go on, she would do even more, in secret. She left me, taking our son and all the household goods with her, and moved to Little Rock, Arkansas. I reluctantly moved in with my grandmother. We had not been married even two years.

When this happened, I was just a few weeks out from the publication of my book and was in the middle of getting the press releases prepared. I lived with my grandmother for the next six months, using that time to hustle even more and save what little money I could to use toward getting myself a place to live, a computer (my wife had taken the home computer with her), some household furnishings, and getting the book published, though I still helped my grandmother with groceries and monthly expenses. I knew if I didn't use that window of time to set up some sort of foundation for myself, and fast, that I would undoubtedly sink even deeper into a widening hole of poverty and future financial problems and post-release depression, which are the typical circumstances for black ex-felons such as myself. I was basically faced with a temporary choice of making those child support and back pay payments or using that money to try to give myself a brighter future so that I could eventually take care of myself as well as my children, long-term. If I could have afforded to do both every month, I certainly would have. But most months it came down to making a choice, and I always made the choice that I thought was the most intelligent one, under the circumstances. At the time, I did not understand that a man can go to jail and serve serious time over missed child support payments.

Once I was able to get my own place (that I had to put in someone else's name because of all the complications and disenfranchisements that come with my ex-felon status) and an old used computer and printer that I found for cheap and was able to get financing for, I finally got the book finalized and published. Then, within just a few days of that, as if on cue to burst my bubble, two more court documents showed up at my grandmother's house for me. One was a summons to again appear in child support court, this time for a contempt of court charge regarding the missed payments to my daughter's mother. The other document revealed that my wife had filed for and been granted a divorce in Arkansas, had claimed I was the one who had abandoned the marriage, and had been granted, in my absence, a court order for child support in the amount of three hundred dollars per month, with a payment being due immediately.

    As for the contempt charge, let me turn back the page for a minute here and give a quick related backstory about the situation with my daughter's mother. As I previously stated, my daughter has never wanted for anything since birth, despite me not being there initially, and her mother has never been poor or without the means to provide for her. Several years before I was released from prison the first time, my daughter's mother and grandmother had opened up a home-based daycare business (which was actually my idea for them to start, not my daughter's mother's or her mother's idea). At that time, my daughter's mother was still living in her mother's home; she first moved out when I came home and we had that apartment I previously mentioned. By the time I got out of prison the second time, she and her mother had several storefront daycare centers that were operational. My daughter's mother had just bought a really nice three thousand square foot home in a new suburb in Memphis. But before she bought that house, *she was receiving state welfare benefits for our daughter, because their daycare business was mostly a cash business and her mother was "paying her" under the table. So as far as the state knew, she was poor.* She had been illegally receiving the benefits from the time my daughter was born up until when she was prepared to buy her house, which is when she voluntarily got off welfare. This means that all or most of that back pay that I owed would go directly to the state, not to her or our daughter. (In situations like this, the law requires that the father of the child in question has to repay the state for providing for his child in his absence.) Once I found out that she had done this, instead of proceeding to report my child's other parent to the authorities to try and have her arrested (I probably couldn't have proven it because there was no paper trail, but I would never do something so lowdown like that to my child's other parent anyway, unlike her), I asked her to take me off of court-ordered child support and leave the courts out of it and just deal with me directly, which she flat out refused and has refused several more times since then.

When I went to court on the contempt charge and had my chance to talk, I tried being completely honest about my situation, which I quickly learned was the worst thing I could have done. I explained everything to the judge about my situation and told him that I only missed the payments so that I could prop myself up financially to be able to make consistent future payments, and more, for the long-term. I explained that it was a short-term necessity that could not be avoided under the circumstances and that I could prove that by showing my income and expenses. I also explained that I was being denied access to my daughter and that her last name still had not been changed. It was a complete shock to me that the judge then, seemingly gleefully, used my statements against me in order to justify finding me guilty of contempt of court, and told me that I had a few hours to come up with six hundred dollars or I would be receiving a six-month jail sentence and would be remanded to the custody of the county jail that day. He said that I admitted to having the money in my possession to make the payments but had chosen not to. Though there were many ways he could have chosen to interpret what I had said to him, he chose to interpret it in a way that could justify punitive action against me.

  When that judge (a white male Republican, by the way) began to say those things to me, all I could think about was how this "family court" proceeding starkly reminded me of criminal court, where the focus rightfully tends to be on the levying of punitive consequences for committing clearly criminal/antisocial actions. Yet, here I was, in family court, once again being treated like a criminal and threatened with a steel cage, but this time for not having enough money. *After having served twelve years in federal prison and being for the most part systematically disenfranchised and legally disqualified from making a living the way most people in society make a living (a job), here I was being penalized even further, financially and physically, by a court, for not being able to make a living.* I got on the phone and borrowed the money from my mother, made the payment, and left that courthouse determined to never enter it or any other courthouse ever again, for any reason.

Ironically and yet inevitably, this was not the last time I would not be able to make some of my child support payments. Once I was put on child support by my wife too, things got even more rough for me for a time. Over the next year or so, there were many months when I just didn't have it. There were months when I didn't really have it but still managed to pay something on it, but had to go without gas or food money for a week. There were many months when I paid one child support payment but couldn't afford to pay the other. As I recall, at that point in my life I was playing catchup in at least a dozen different ways. I really was in the most vulnerable state one can be in in our society: black, male, had been incarcerated for a very long time during my formative adult years, on five years of probation (which comes with its own set of rules and limitations and fees), broke, labeled an ex-felon by federal, state and local governments and thus barred from being able to get what most people would call a "good job" or even a shelf stocking job at Walmart, no work experience to put on a résumé, and in debt on several different fronts under strict and punitive terms and conditions. It is an understatement to say that it would not be easy for any person to adjust to society and make a decent living for themselves while under these circumstances.

   And as many former inmates will tell you, the stress that comes with living in free society is sometimes worse than the stress of being physically locked up inside of prison, and especially so when you have served a long stretch of time. You must learn and relearn just about everything, even the smallest stuff that most people take for granted, and you are years behind everyone else on pretty much everything with very little to nothing in your favor. (When I first came home from prison and drove a car, I remember nearly getting myself killed by getting onto the expressway *on the off ramp* one time, confused about how to drive on the expressway. I remember not knowing how to put gas in a car at first.) So, after spending all that time locked up in steel cages and concrete boxes all across the country, here I was trying to start multiple businesses and a family and juggle all the many requirements and big responsibilities and deadlines that come with living "free" in society as an ex-felon. It's living under constant scrutiny and pressure with much fewer opportunities than most others but with very little room for error, to say the least. So yes, I missed more payments and eventually, due to the twelve percent interest that accrues on child support arrears in Tennessee, my child support debt reached over fifteen thousand dollars before I was able to resume making both child support payments on a consistent basis. (During that period of hard time, I still did get summoned to court several times and told to make lump sum payments, or go to jail. I had my driver's license suspended a few times, credit ruined, and was never eligible to get a passport.)

Yet, compared to the stories of most black ex-felons who have had to deal with the child support system, my own story is a walk in the park. I cite my own personal experience with the child support system in this first chapter just to show one example of how uncaringly the system typically handles black men and black families and the negative effects that usually result from it, but there are thousands more examples that can be cited by others that have had far worse outcomes than mine. As you can see, I had lots of help in the beginning when I first came home and was eventually able to become a financially stable self-employed entrepreneur. I was luckily able to avoid actually being re-incarcerated over child support issues, and that's mainly because of that help from others. This is not the case for most black men who come from where I come from, as most of them don't have the help available to them that I had. But it almost doesn't matter whether you are an ex-felon or not when dealing with the child support system; oftentimes black men who are unemployed or underemployed get hit with unfair stipulations and conditions that eventually lead to all kinds of punitive restrictions being placed on their lives, as well as incarceration. There are probably several hundreds of thousands of black men in America who have had extremely negative experiences with the child support system, for one reason or another, and who will tell you that the system has a way of turning a potentially amicable family situation into something bad or making an already bad family situation, worse. In fact, I've met very few black men who have had anything good at all to say about the child support system and the way it conducts business when it comes to them, their children, and their family situations. So, since I believe that it matters greatly what black men think, especially when it comes to issues that directly affect us and our families, it is my position that our general perspective on this particular issue needs to be succinctly and thoroughly explained and exposed, to the world. That is why I decided to write this book.

  At the time of this book's writing, I have now been out of prison for over thirteen years and I still only have two children—my daughter Oryanna, and my son Michael. When I was first released from prison, my daughter was two years old; Oryanna is now an almost grown teenager in high school, and I have not seen her alone since her mother found out I had gotten married. My daughter's last name has not been changed and she now calls her mother's new husband "Daddy" and has rebuffed or ignored every attempt I have ever made to contact her or communicate with her. As far as I know, she knows nothing about my life circumstances or the real story on the relationship I had with her mother. I don't have any idea what her mother has told her about me, but judging by her actions, it can't be too good. And now, because of all the hostility that has been unnecessarily sewn into the situation by her mother, my daughter does not know me, does not know where I live, and has not even met her great-grandmother on my side of the family, who looks like her much older twin and is ninety-three years old and counting, as I write this. Even though my daughter seemingly does not want to know me or know where I live, the really sad part is that even if she did, because of how her mother has influenced her, I honestly would be paranoid about that because I would subconsciously be worried that she would potentially be reporting back to her mother anything that she could use to hurt me or have child support services and law enforcement constantly at my door over the unrighteous debt I owe to the state of Tennessee. Where there is no trust there can be no relationship, and there is no way that I could trust my daughter's mother after she has tried on multiple occasions to have me locked back up in a cage, over money, and has kept our child from me and my family for so long. So, as a result, today, we have no relationship whatsoever. And all because I didn't want to be with her and married someone else, nearly four years after *she* had made the decision to end the relationship we had.

    I really regret that I have not been able to help mold my daughter's character and mindset and teach her those things that she needs to know that no one else is fully qualified to teach her like her real father is, and even from a distance I can see the negative effects of that. I have been secretly following her on social media since she became a teen, and some of the things I have seen are not encouraging at all. Even at age fifteen, she unabashedly cursed like a sailor, bragged about not doing well in school, and regularly talked about sexual acts, drugs, and stealing and seemed to already have a penchant for thuggish gangbanging gun-toting boys that were much older than herself. At the age of fifteen, she was even openly "friends" with several XXX-rated porn sites on Instagram. Judging by her social media activity, one could easily surmise that, at the least, she isn't being properly supervised by her mother and quite possibly is being brought up in a very unhealthy and irresponsible manner, just like I was as a small child and teen while living with my mother. But because of missed child support payments, I'm the parent that has been mislabeled by the system as the "bad parent" in the situation—just like my real father was once labeled the same, for the same reason. (In my own upbringing, my mother physically and emotionally abused me for the first fifteen years of my childhood and introduced me to the very worst sides of life on a daily basis and was never held responsible for any of it. I was raised in a project household where my young mother and crack smoking stepfather, whom she raised me to call "Daddy," physically fought on a weekly basis, carelessly had sex and did drugs in front of me, barely ever had enough food, and beat on me like I was an unwanted mistake whose crime was existence. Yet, my real father was the one who was labeled and disregarded as a "deadbeat" parent by the system and everyone who was on the outside looking in, because of a few missed child support payments. While my mother was socially regarded as a victim, for the most part. As she got older my mother changed for the better, and I've long since forgiven her for everything that happened in my childhood, but that does not change what happened or erase the negative effects that came from it.)

What happened in my situation with my daughter's mother is an example of exactly the type of emotion-based vengeful vitriol that is all too typical in today's times when dealing with the various issues of child support stemming from the breakup of relationships. And, again, the data clearly shows that when courts get involved they tend to make things worse, not better,[5] and especially so when it comes to black families. I personally believe that these negative effects are, for the most part, the unstated intent of the child support system when it comes to black families, not mere coincidence or happenstance or regrettable effects of good-intended bad policy. *The rules and policies of the child support system, coupled with a shown penchant and reputation for dealing especially harshly with poor black male defendants, has everything to do with these widespread effects. Thus, the system is certainly sometimes viewed and used as a potential tool for vengeful actions by many upset black females who want to place their child's father in harm's way because they are angry with him for reasons that have nothing to do with him being a father to his children.* In past times, before the current child support systems were put into place in America, courts didn't act as if they had to force parents to be parents, and they didn't get involved just because they could. Today, they get involved just because they can. If a child support order is requested today, by either a parent or the state, a child support order will be handed down nearly one hundred percent of the time. *A child support order is really a contract between the defendant and the courts, not between the parents.* So, today, to be on child support is akin to being on parole or probation for a crime that has not yet been committed. (See Chapter Five for additional info on this subject area.)

  Now, for argument's sake, let's flip the scenario and look at what some may think are three controversial choices I made in my situation and see what potentially could have happened had I chosen to do these three things differently. Those three choices were: my actions in the halfway house with respect to starting a business vs. getting a low-paying manual labor job; my actions and nonactions with regard to my daughter's mother and court; and my choice to miss some initial child support payments in order to set myself up to be able to provide more in the future. First, if I had just been satisfied with getting a job when I first came home, the typical type of job that ex-felons who have spent over ten years in prison would get, I would still have had the initial issues I had but there would have been even more issues later on down the line. No job that I could have gotten would have sustained me even as much as my cleaning contracts did, and I would have been working longer, harder hours for less money. In the beginning, when I was soliciting and getting contracts for my cleaning business and using my spare time to work on my book, if I had had a job I would not have been able to complete any of that book-related stuff until much later, if at all. Also, with my wife working the way she was, our family would not have been able to function because I would not have been able to watch and take care of the kids' needs like I did and we certainly could not have afforded child care.

Secondly, with regard to my daughter's mother, some of you may ask why I didn't just take her to court, to which I say, just think about that for a minute, and try to put yourself in my shoes at the time. "Court" hasn't exactly been an inviting place for me in my life, and it's not just me; many, if not most, black men feel the exact same way. One out of every three black men living in America today have either been to jail or have been on probation or parole in their lifetime,[6] and most of them have children. How many of them do you think want to go to court, voluntarily, knowing that they are (and have been in the past) vulnerable to all kinds of problems that could come from that courtroom encounter that involves hostile prosecutors and hostile judges with hostile tools at their disposal to potentially use against them? I think a better question to ask would be why, especially considering my circumstances, did *she* take *me* to court in the first place? And the honest answer to that question is, only because she was mad at me, *not* because it was actually necessary to get me to support and be a father to my child.

If my daughter's mother had been even mildly reasonable, we could have worked everything out without any court intervention, to an end that truly was in our child's best interest and with her own probable future desires in mind. *In that courtroom, neither the judge, prosecutor, or my daughter's mother had the child's long-term best interest at heart.* In the end, it turns out that my daughter's mother didn't really care much about me "supporting" our daughter in any way other than financially because since that time she has done everything possible to keep me from having a meaningful relationship with Oryanna, including possibly turning her against me. Really, if you ask me, I don't think she cared much about the financial part either—the totality of her actions after I was released from prison clearly shows that she just wanted to hurt me in the only way she could, without regard for how it trickles down and hurts and affects our daughter. Would it have been worth the risk to take her to court over it? Maybe. Maybe not. At the time, with all that was going on in my life, my only thoughts were about how unnecessary it all was and that I didn't want to be inside of a courtroom facing another hostile judge ever again. I thought, "What if the judge wants to focus on my debt to the state or my missed payments? What if things take a turn for the worse and I get further penalized? What if I get locked up for this reason, or that reason?" Plus, when my daughter's mother first started acting crazy, I did not think it would last as long as it has. I figured she would "come around" at some point after some time passed and that in the meantime I would be preparing myself to be ready whenever she did. But to this day, she hasn't.

    Thirdly, with regard to the child support payments that I missed while I was attempting to get myself together, there is no doubt in my mind that if I had not missed those payments early on that I would almost certainly have gone to jail for missed payments later on. Most times that I missed payments I really couldn't help it because I just didn't have the money, but some others I chose to miss because I had to choose between making that monthly payment or putting it toward something urgent that needed to be done to get my business off the ground as soon as possible. As I've said, at the time I fully understood that if I was going to establish myself as an entrepreneur I would have to make some sacrifices and take certain risks and that, if successful, it would pay off big-time in the end and everything would work out fine. And I was right. The reason I am where I am and can do what I do today is because of how I did what I did back then.

Had the fragility of my life circumstances been on the table to be considered in court, with a little good faith and wisdom applied, I would have been afforded some initial much-needed leeway to establish a social and financial foothold in society before being placed under a potentially crippling financial burden, and that would have been better for both me and my daughter because a lot of things would have happened differently after that. If the judge had bothered to inquire as to the immediate needs of the child at that time and the mother's financial ability to provide for her alone for a short time (the same way she took care of her alone while I was in prison) vs. what my needs were in order to get the ball rolling whereas I could get myself established enough to begin contributing consistently and abundantly, things would certainly have worked out better for all involved, especially our child. But these fundamental elements of the situation were never taken into consideration by the court. All that was considered was whether I was the father and how much I was to pay and how much I owed already. That's it. As if we were robots and not people with mitigating life circumstances that may need to be taken into consideration within the process, *for the long-term best interest of the child.*

  Every situation is different; if my child was in need and her mother was not in a position to handle things herself financially for a short time, then requiring me to begin monthly payments immediately, irrespective of my circumstances, would have been reasonable and justifiable. But my child's mother was making nice money, much more than I was making, and was living in a three thousand square foot home and was operating two successful daycare centers. I, on the other hand, had nothing but the gigantic odds that were stacked against me, and a dream. Still, I was ordered to not only begin making immediate monthly payments, but back pay as well, for the time I was in prison after my daughter was born. I am just thankful that I was lucky and fortunate enough to be able to not fall victim to the system in the worst ways possible, the way many other black men have. Because, system-wise, it was seemingly set up for that to be the most likely outcome for people "like me" from the start.

  As for my son and his mother, my ex-wife, they are still living in Arkansas and doing well. We still keep in touch and have no issues whatsoever. A couple of years after they left Memphis, my son was diagnosed with autism. Though she had originally gone to the courts and had me placed on child support when she first left, not long after he was diagnosed she went back to the court and had me taken off of court supervised payments. Since then, I've sent her money every month, like I would have done anyway without the initial involvement of the child support system. When the diagnosis happened, she said that she realized how important good co-parenting would be in our situation with Michael and admitted that she initially had me placed on court-ordered child support mostly out of anger and frustration and *not* because she felt it was really necessary. My take on it was that co-parenting would have been just as important had our son not been autistic and that she never should have left our marriage in the first place. However, I knew that the real reason she left was because she was suffering from postpartum depression that was largely due to financial uncertainty and strain, and I consider that to be my fault to a large degree. (Even though she should've known from the beginning, especially as an ex-employee of the Bureau of Prisons, that it would not be easy for an ex-prisoner after serving over a decade in prison.) That aside, I was just glad that she had that realization before too much time had passed and before more bad energy was developed between us that would have undoubtedly adversely affected our son in some ways.

But I have to ask: How many times do you think the same sort of things I've described that happened with my situations, happen in today's "baby mama/baby daddy" culture of the black community? Again, from the research I have conducted, anger and frustration and revenge are among the most typical reasons black men are placed on court-ordered child support, *not* the fact that black men are by and large deadbeat dads who don't want to take care of their own children, as certain racist stereotypes about black men and court-ordered child support can suggest. Long before the child support system was the staple in the black community that it is today, black men in America were by and large taking care of their children. Black men, even as slaves, sought to care for and raise their children. The black man once was lauded as the head of the black family; now, in many if not most cases, the black family is headed by a "system" or a non-caring judge in a courtroom who has the final say on what happens or doesn't happen with regard to the family and child. Now they have convinced many people that black fathers need a punitive system, one that was created by racist white men and white feminists, to police and monitor their parenting in the event the relationship that produced the child fails, to supposedly protect the interest and wellbeing of the black child and black mother. Yet, the typical outcome when the system intervenes is more damage being done to the future wellbeing of all parties involved, especially the children.

As for me, I am happy to have been continuously "free" for nearly fourteen years straight. And I intend to keep it that way for the rest of my life. I am not a criminal (as far as I am concerned, I never really was). I am now in my mid-forties, and a totally different guy than that young dumb teenager who naively sold dope and got busted and went to jail. I'm a guy who thinks totally different from the younger me who thought it was okay to hang around with people who were into certain negative things that I was not into, as long as I did not indulge in it myself. I know better than that now. I know how to avoid all of those things, today. Yet and still, from the very first month that I stepped foot out of prison that second time, I have been under constant threat of re-incarceration, but not for committing crimes. That threat comes from the U.S. child support system—the only area in my life where the real prospect of me returning to a prison cell has been a viable possibility. Which is why I decided to write this book. I believe there are many women who have children with black men who don't understand the true auspices of putting their children's fathers under the authority and control of "the system." Because the truth is, *none of the standing systems of America that were designed by state and federal governments, which are and always have been predominately controlled by racist white males, have ever had black people's best interest at heart, and that is a fact.*

Therefore, with this book, I aim to showcase just how the current child support system is failing black families and render real and sensible suggestions on what needs to be done about it. From a black father's perspective.

CHAPTER TWO

A Summary on When, Why, & How U.S. Child Support Laws Were Created

"If you would understand anything, observe it's beginning and development."
– Aristotle[7]

The child support system as we know it today is fairly young when compared to many of our other institutionalized public service systems in America. Established in 1975,[8] The current child support system was purportedly envisioned and designed based on a stated bipartisan desire to reduce welfare expenses and financially mediate between divorced or otherwise separated parents. Previous to 1975 there had been in place a government entitlement program called Aid to Families with Dependent Children (AFDC), which was a part of the Social Security Act, that had been enacted in 1935 to help *white* children who were in extremely poor or low-income families. Both of these programs, though enacted forty years apart, were steeped in vestige principles and practices of former times; times when fathers were typically expected to be the sole breadwinners for their families and good opportunities within the workforce for women were extremely limited. Therefore, most wives and mothers were expected to be dependent homemakers and mainly focused on child rearing duties. These were very different realities from what typically exists today, and therein lies the crux of the problem. The child support system that exists today is fundamentally the exact same system as the previous ones—it is based on many of those same outdated principles that were formed over forty years ago and earlier, with very few for-the-better changes being made to it over the years. (Nearly all the changes made to the system since 1975 have been punitive in nature.) To say that the system is outdated and thus inefficient by today's standards is indeed an understatement. A total overhaul of the child support system with well-intended, well-researched, modernized policy is sorely needed.

The legal definition of child support is basically "funds ordered by the court for one parent to pay to the other to assist equitably in the cost of raising their shared children."[9] Simply put, "support" is, most often, defined and determined by a standardized table that factors in the number of children, the income of one or both parents, and the custody arrangement. Finances are and always have been the main focus of what is considered "child support" in America, even before 1935.[10] The notion of child support in the U.S. was first raised in the early nineteenth century,[11] when convoluted courts that were dealing with voluminous cases of divorce and marital breakdowns found that the laws didn't have provisions for post-marriage financial child support. From its inception, America had inherited many of its domestic laws from England and many of those laws were still wholly in place in the late eighteenth and early nineteenth centuries, with few deviations having been made to them. With respect to parental support of children, those inherited laws held that fathers only had a non-enforceable moral duty to provide support for their children. The law-creating bodies of those past eras seemed to seek to keep what they considered to be "family business" out of the jurisdiction of the law and courts. In fact, most English legal precedents actually forbade a third party from even attempting to recover costs of any funds owed for "child support" unless they had a pre-authorized contract for providing such support with the father of the child.[12] At certain points in time, old English laws did sometimes allow for recovery of support expenses from a father. For instance, England's Poor Relief Act[13] law of 1601 authorized local parishes in English territory to recoup funds that were spent on caring for single mothers and their children who hadn't been provided for by their husbands and fathers.

Despite the general absence of child support provisions within old English laws, American courts gradually began to undertake the notion that a father had both a moral *and* legal obligation/duty to support his offspring. The

Supreme Court of Connecticut decided a case in 1808, Stanton vs. Wilson[14], that allowed a woman by the name of Eunice Stanton to recover financial child support for her two children from her first husband on behalf of her second husband, who was deceased at the time the case was brought. The court stated in this case that the children's biological father was indeed legally bound "to protect, educate, and maintain their legitimate children." Several courts in other states also began to assert that a father could indeed be legally held financially responsible for providing for children he sired in a defunct relationship.

Soon after, the issue of child financial dependency came up in nearly every divorce case that was decided by American courts during the nineteenth century, mainly because many newly divorced white mothers during that time were forced to live in poverty. Even families that were middle class or wealthy before the divorce found that, after the divorce, the fathers tended to continue to prosper while the mothers, *because of the social limitations placed on their gender*, usually became insolvent or poor. This typically occurred because the men, due to the divorce, were suddenly set free from the expenses of the family, whereas the women were not. After a divorce, a woman was still considered to be directly responsible for the expenses associated with raising the children. Which meant she had to either find another man to support her and her children, or find work for herself, neither of which were guaranteed to sufficiently provide the support she needed. Even if a divorced mother could find a job during those times, she almost always earned much less than what a man would have brought into the family.

Once the obligation for out-of-home fathers to financially provide for their children began to be established in law, multitudes of early child support claims were being brought by third parties who had provided board, food, or supplies to impoverished single mothers and their children and who were wanting to recover these spent monies from the non-supporting fathers. And as the American child support doctrine continued to be developed (still centrally around the old-world notion that fathers would be the only or main breadwinners), the courts began using a simple two-part "test" to determine the basis for child support reimbursement from absentee fathers. First, the courts sought to determine if the things that were provided by the plaintiff were indeed things that the child needed at the time they were given. Second, the courts would try to determine if the father had really been negligent in providing his offspring with those needed items himself. American courts then began utilizing this new child support doctrine to allow divorced women to recover monies directly from their ex-spouses for the support of their offspring. Litigating mothers not only had to prove the ex-husbands had failed to support their own children, but also needed to prove that their spouse was at fault for the dissolution of the marriage. Still, barring any mitigating circumstances, the father was only obligated to pay the minimal cost of the bare maintenance of the child. By the late 1800's, nearly every state in the country had some legally enforceable duty for a father to *financially* support his children on the books. (It is important for me to reiterate that the child support system that was being developed during these times was for white women and white families only—not blacks. Slavery didn't allow blacks to be married under the law, nor did it allow black males to be considered head of household. Under slavery, black children did not have a legal father, so there was no way that a black mother could seek compensation from her children's father. It wasn't until long after the Civil War *and* Reconstruction had ended that black men and women slowly began gaining the legal parental and custodial rights and duties that could make seeking court-ordered child support even possible for them.[15])

Child support mission statements, policies, and laws would begin to be more punitively developed during the twentieth century, whilst keeping most of the outdated foundational aspects firmly in place. Congress passed the first federal child support enforcement legislation in 1950,[16] which required all state welfare agencies to immediately contact law enforcement whenever they had to provide aid to dependent children who had reportedly been abandoned by a parent. Then, Social Security Act amendments in 1965 allowed local and state welfare agencies to glean information from the Secretary of Health, Education and Welfare (now the Department of Health and Human Services) detailing the personal addresses and all places of employment of non-custodial parents who owed court-ordered child support.[17] Then in 1975 Title IV-D of the Social Security Act was signed into law, which allowed the Department of Health and Human Services to establish a separate watchdog departmental division that would be dedicated to supervising the operation of a national child support enforcement program.[18] This new enforcement program established three things: a parent locator service, mandatory operational guidelines for states, and plans for periodic reviews of cases. Each state retained the primary responsibility to operate the program within its own borders.

Then, in 1984, the Child Support Enforcement amendments followed, which required that every state develop mandatory income withholding procedures as well as strict processes for enforcing child support orders (such as wage confiscation, income tax refund interceptions, property seizures and property liens[19]). These punitive amendments also empowered states to report delinquent parents and their child support debt to consumer credit agencies. A while later, The Family Support Act of 1988[20] was adopted and enacted, which required the courts to use state guidelines when calculating child support payouts and required all states to review their guidelines every four years. Another important child support provision was established with the enactment of the Child Recovery Act of 1992,[21] which made it a federal crime to purposefully fail to pay past-due child support payments in cases where a child resides in another state, whereas it's a state crime if the child resides in the same state as the non-custodial parent. It's worth mentioning that "purposefully fail" within that context is solely and subjectively left up to prosecutors and judges to determine.

In America today, all noncustodial parents, the overwhelming majority of whom are men, are legally liable and obligated to pay child support. Which would be a good thing, if the system was set up right. But the way the system has been set up to work, it is doing more harm than good, especially for those men who are poor like a large percentage of black men are. (Due to racism-based income inequality, the percentage of adult black men in poverty has always been at least double that of adult white men.[22]) For the poor and disenfranchised, statistics show that being involved with the child support system only works toward compounding their poverty.[23] Under the Obama administration, there were some efforts made by the government to change certain aspects of national child support policy that was causing this compounding of poverty. Both the Obama administration and the Commissioner for the Office of Child Support Enforcement, Vicki Turetsky, were very outspoken about the need for policy changes concerning noncustodial parents who cannot afford to pay child support, but those efforts pretty much fell on deaf ears. Then, in 2011, there was a Supreme Court ruling mandating that lower courts keep parents out of jail unless they are sure that person can actually pay the debt,[24] but most conservative politicians were and still are against the idea, claiming it undercuts the value and purpose of personal responsibility. When the Obama administration proposed a new approach to the child support system that would do away with harsh burdens being placed on poor non-custodial parents, Senator Orrin Hatch of Utah was among the loudest conservative voices that claimed it was a bad idea. "Deadbeat parents, not hardworking taxpayers, should be held accountable for their financial responsibilities," he said in a press release.[25] But in-the-know pros like Ms. Turetsky strongly disagreed with that sentiment, saying it's not that simple at all. "Jail is appropriate for someone who is actively hiding assets, not appropriate for someone who couldn't pay the order in the first place," Turetsky told the New York Times in 2015.[26] I, personally, would add a caveat to Turetsky's statement: Jail is appropriate for someone who is actively hiding assets...*and who does not provide sufficient support (sufficient as defined by social norms, not skewed politicized courts) for their offspring.*

So, as I've said, even with all the amendments and many additions that have been made to the U.S. child support system over the past two hundred years, the irony is that it is still very much an outdated system that needs many more elemental changes to bring it to where it needs to be in order for it to be able to rightly address today's highly variable parental situations and circumstances, especially with respect to the poor and disenfranchised. Policy-wise, America is evidently willing to accept extremely high rates of single mother parentage within its society because it continuously lacks the political will to enact good social policies that would truly support such families, including workplace childcare and some form of national maternity leave; things which have been commonplace in many other countries for a long time. Yet, America has no problem whatsoever with creating and upholding a punitive system with punitive policies that effectively bolster the levels of single mother parentage, helping to create a dangerous new social reality that normalizes broken homes, fatherless children, and enmity between parents. The fact is, there are much better alternatives and solutions to what's being done currently with regard to the child support system, some of which are outlined in this book. My only hope is that at some point people of good faith, after being made aware of all the facts involved, will demand changes and those changes are subsequently brought to bear.

CHAPTER THREE

Child Support and The Black Family: What We Need from The System vs. What We Get

"Do I not destroy my enemies when I make them my friends?"
— Abraham Lincoln[27]

"A fake friend can cause much more damage than a real enemy." — Unknown

The black family in America is in a full-blown state of crisis. Fully intact black families are on a steep decline and have been for some time.[28] Black marriage is on the decline. Responsible black fatherhood is on the decline. Responsible black motherhood is on the decline. So much so, that people have started to redefine what a family actually entails and truly is. Yes, it's been proven that you can have a happy family with no father in the home. Yes, it's been proven that you can have a happy family with no mother present. Yes, you can even have a happy family with no children at all. But who would argue that the best-case scenario, especially from the average child's perspective, isn't to have a happy family with both parents in the home? And if that isn't possible, to have the parents operating congenially and civilly with each other with the child having equal access to both parents, not some court-ordered "every other weekend" monitored or unmonitored timed "visitation" type deal that is so typical with child support orders? Some adults may selfishly want to make that argument, but I seriously doubt that many children would. So first and foremost, let us consider the black child's point of view when it comes to certain current child support policies and practices and how they tend to negatively affect the black family, which is a point of view that is seemingly rarely ever taken into true consideration by parents or the courts when they are litigating these issues.

At any given time, black children make up between fifteen and twenty percent of all children in America, and make up about thirty percent of the total black American population.[29] Currently, that roughly amounts to about fifteen million black children, with nearly seventy percent of them being raised by single mothers.[30] Most black children in America are born "out of wedlock,"[31] which could mean many things, but typically means they were born under circumstances where there was either no meaningful relationship between the parents or the parents were in a relationship but the child wasn't conceived under ideal circumstances. (I can say this because the overwhelming majority of black people in America do strongly believe in marriage; nearly ninety percent of blacks in America are religious,[32] and for religious people marriage is a religious act. In the black community especially, relationships are not typically considered "official" unless marriage either happens or is planned to happen at some point.) Since statistics show that nearly seventy percent of America's black children are, on any given day, in "single mother households," this does show that these "single" mothers are not married, but does not suggest that they aren't dealing with men sexually and in other ways, which is likely true for the great majority of them. However, they typically are *not* dealing closely with the father(s) of their child or children, other than through the court system. This seems to be the visible standard operating procedure now in black America, and maybe even America in general, when relationships end and children are involved.

I've known many single black women with children in my life, some of them being family members, and very few of them were not consistently or periodically having some sort of close relations with at least one male who was not the actual father of their child or children. So, when it comes to all these "single" mothers with kids, many times it's not that their child or children are not being privy to some version of male parental energy and/or even support, it's that the children typically are not going to develop life-long parent-child bonds with boyfriends of the mothers who don't either marry her or stay with her for at least five to ten years, minimum. And we know that most relationships do not last that long these days, especially when compared to the era when the question of child support was first raised in court. (Data on today's relationships show a steep decline in the average length of time they tend to last.[33]) And many times, when it comes to relationships with men who are not the biological father of their kid(s), women typically find that men tend to move on after the relationship ends and do not continue to treat and support their children the same way they did when they were in the relationship, hence one reason for the popularized cliché "treat you like a stepchild." Most of these men probably have children of their own to support, and may go on to be in relationships with other women who already have or will have children, just as a woman may end up being with other men who would then also be in her kid(s) life. Again, the pervasive trend in this day and age is that once a breakup happens, the biological parents become virtual enemies to each other, while getting into relationships with other people, oftentimes repeating that same cycle over and over again. Why is this scenario so prevalent, in today's times? And does anyone care about how this particular type of trending negative family activity tends to affect the children that are involved, in the long run? How is normalizing this type of behavior influencing the kids who are caught in the middle of these type of situations?

   I believe that boys and girls react to this sort of thing differently in many cases, but I think it's safe to say that, at the very least, boys and girls both are subconsciously being taught that this is just the way things are handled in relationships. Which normalizes this behavior in their eyes and greatly heightens the likelihood that they will continue those same sorts of practices and habits once they get into relationships themselves as adults. (Statistics show that children of broken homes tend to create broken homes themselves as adults and are much more likely to have emotional issues, drug habits, tend to be more critical in their personal relationships and much more derogatory toward other people, etc.[34]) The alternative to this is not only better choice-making on the part of individuals, but also us as a society coming up with better systemic ways of dealing with familial problems that don't tend to make things worse than they already are. For the typical child that is being raised by a single parent who is receiving court-ordered child support, the argument can be made that the system has not served to make their life better in any way other than financially, and not even in that way in many cases. The reason for this is, they are not getting the "support" they really need most because courts are really only concerned with two elements of child "support": money from the noncustodial parent, and punishment for the noncustodial parent for not providing enough of it or not having enough of it, based on its calculations. Yet, I would be willing to bet my last dollar that the typical child would attribute greater value to quality time spent with their father than to any other form of support. But the courts, for some reason, obviously do not concur with that valuation.

The relevant legal definition of the word "support," according to Merriam-Webster's dictionary, is "to provide with substantiation; to pay the cost of; to promote the interests or cause of; to provide a basis for the existence or subsistence of; to hold up or serve as a foundation or prop for." So, what *really* constitutes "supporting" a child in the real world? Let's take a hard look at this question. Can you be considered to be supporting your child if you are extremely poor and cannot provide nutritional meals on a regular basis? Are you supporting your child if you cannot afford to pay for their college education, at a time when college is the most expensive it has ever been yet having a college degree is almost a necessity in order to be well-placed in the job market and the lack of one tends to be a big indicator of probable poverty, especially for black folk? What about if you have a legal drug habit, like smoking tobacco or marijuana or drinking alcohol excessively, and your children see it and are around it? What about women who give birth to drug addicted babies; are they sent to prison and then required to pay child support to the state if their child is taken from them for "unsupportive" behavior? (A 2015 Reuters report titled *The Most Vulnerable Victims of America's Opioid Epidemic: Helpless & Hooked*, states that every nineteen minutes a child is born addicted to opioids in America.[35] 2018 stats are poised to be even worse.) What about if you live in a terrible environment, like the projects or a gang-infested neighborhood, and you do not make continuous efforts to move out of the area—is that "supporting" your children? What if your underage child regularly sees or hears you having sex, like so many children really do (research this on YouTube and you'll see countless examples), is that "supporting" your child? What if you are just an ignorant person who had children but you can't and don't teach them anything worthwhile, which happens all the time—are you supporting them? Arguably the answer is no in all of these scenarios, yet, I can say this: if any of these sorts of things are considered to not be "supporting" a child properly and there was a system specifically set up to monitor and go after parents who commit such offenses, most American children would be put into foster homes and most parents would be dragged into court and would have to serve some time in jail.

The fact is, support is an admixture of things of near-equal value. Love, your physical presence, your guidance, your familial ties, as well as your ability to provide financially are all equally important. *Especially in the eyes of children.* So why is the only element of child "support" that is punishable by harassment and imprisonment, the financial element? Why aren't men who are put into the child support system punitively punished in the same way for not spending enough time with their children? Why aren't parents punished in that same way for not teaching their children certain basic things and for not being actively involved in the daily curricular and extra-curricular activities of their children? Why are parents not similarly punished for not protecting their children or preventing their children from joining gangs or doing drugs or failing miserably in school for no good reason? *Morally, the duty to provide monies to go toward the financial support of a child goes hand in hand with the right and duty of all parents to provide substantial love and time to the child, and to be directly involved in the daily upbringing of the child.* The current child support system, with its incredibly strong legal powers to make liable parents pay regardless, could at least be systematically balanced so that it also mandates both parents and their children to maintain as much contact as possible, which results in a meaningful bond and relationship that has the potential to bear ripe fruit for a lifetime, as well as less money that has to change hands between parents. There is currently no such balance within the system. Family courts tend to make custody and access issues vague and uncertain, and as a result many liable parents end up with no meaningful relationship with the children they are nevertheless required to pay for.

With these sorts of unrefined practices, the government via the child support system is grossly violating long-proven essential aspects of successful human family relationships. The right and duty of the liable noncustodial parent to care for their own children in non-financial ways is not balanced out in law with the responsibility of that parent to pay monies for the physical maintenance of the child. In my view, the integrity and long-term best interests of families where the parents aren't together and live apart should be protected by *ensuring* that both parents have equal or near-equal roles in providing love and time for their children, that parallels their roles in providing finances for their children. The importance of this really cannot be understated. Without this much-needed balance being melded into support rulings and truly enforced by child support policies and laws, with some forms of punitive measures being attached to them if necessary, one parent will usually get subjugated by the other. And in the overwhelming majority of cases, that subjugated parent is the father. Therefore, this balancing is sorely needed and is better, in the short run as well as the long run, for all involved—the children, the parents, and the taxpayers.

Over the years there have been a few state legislative efforts made to attempt to correct the rampant problem of post-relationship parental/custodial imbalance (like introducing what are typically called "shared parenting" bills) but few have been successful, for reasons that are really unclear. There are many "unclear" aspects to the child support system relating to the motivations behind some of the bad policies and procedures that have been enacted and good policies and procedures that have not been enacted. Nevertheless, even with all of its flaws, the child support system exists and arguably needs to exist, because there indeed are parents who do run from their parental responsibilities. Though I tend to believe that "deadbeat" parents who actively run from their parental responsibilities are the exceptions to the rule and not the rule, like certain current child support system data and practices indirectly suggests that a large number of black men are.

So, with all that I have pointed out, what then does the black family need from the U.S. child support system? Generally speaking, in my opinion, there are two main things. *The first thing the black family needs more than anything is for the system to not serve as a wedge maker between parents who may be at odds with one another for reasons that have nothing to do with anyone not providing child support, and to stop getting involved, just because it can, in black family business when it is not necessary.* One parent filing a legal complaint about child support should not automatically necessitate a court order or judgement eventually being issued against the other parent. A merit-based hearing should be had first to determine whether due negligence is actually occurring in the first place, *with a mandate to refuse court intervention if not.* That alone would rectify many of the problems that come with government intervention in black family affairs. It would undoubtedly result in less of everything that is wrong with the system—less parent on parent abuse, less parent on child abuse, fewer situations where children are used as pawns to exact revenge or inflict pain on the other parent, and less abuse of the financial aspects of child support where over-payment for the actual costs of child rearing can be greatly exaggerated against men of means. (Example - the rapper 50 Cent has paid nearly one and half million dollars in child support,[36] for one child. The mother allegedly spent the money on many things that had nothing to do with their son, with no legal accountability for it whatsoever. We all know it doesn't take nearly that amount of money to raise a child for eighteen years. The mother of his son allegedly did not earn even one-third of that amount herself during that entire time period, so there's no way she could have equally financially contributed to their son's upbringing what 50 was mandated to contribute. Still, 50 Cent would have faced jail time if he had decided to, say, only give her a million dollars, even though in actuality that still would've been more money than most people would spend to raise ten children and more than the mother contributed.)

Speaking of 50 Cent, his situation with his oldest son and the mother is just another prime example of how the system can be and is abused by many women who really should not have been able to file a child support case and get a judgement in the first place. The court's one-sided intervention seemingly further drove a wedge into their family situation that has not been repaired to date. First, the court forced 50 Cent to pay her an absurd amount of money every month, allegedly without ever establishing that 50 Cent was a bad father who was not taking care of his child. If the court would have been allowed to refuse even hearing the case, based on the fact that 50 Cent was already sufficiently providing for his son *as he sees fit* (which is supposed to be the right of all parents, whether they are together or not, as long as needs are being met and there is no abuse of any sort), that would have made greater the chances that he and the mother would interact better and work together more down the line, for the benefit of their son. But when the court steps in at her behest and basically tells her that it is forcing 50 Cent, under penalty of incarceration, to give her an obscene amount of money that she can do anything she wants with, it predictably empowered and emboldened her to further become and remain his enemy.

This sort of thing happens to black men on all levels, not just to rich men like 50 Cent. It happened to me! I'm convinced that many, if not most, black men who have been put into the child support system by their child's mother did not need to be; they would have taken care of their offspring regardless, as most black men did before there was ever a such thing as a child support system. Many would have done even more than they were required to do by the courts, if they had just been left alone by the courts. In the early days of 50 Cent's career, his oldest son was his pride and joy and it wasn't hard to tell. The movie about his life, *Get Rich or Die Tryin*, shows how involved and loving he was with his son before the split from the mother occurred. Now, allegedly thanks to the mother's hyper-negative energy and influence, which in my opinion was spurred on by the court's looming one-sided influence, 50 Cent's son wants nothing to do with him and thinks him a bad person because of the situation with his mother.[37] The same thing was true in my case; my daughter was the apple of my eye that I cherished spending time with and looked forward to doing fatherly things for until her mother vengefully ran to the courts and had me put under undue punitive financial pressure and began doing everything she could do to deny my right to be a hands-on father, including turning my daughter against me. *When parents become enemies, it is never good for the child or children that are involved.* And one of the surefire ways to make the average black man in America your enemy is to unnecessarily and vengefully put him under the punitive racist authority of the courts of America. In 50 Cent's case, the result that came from his son's mother doing these things to him is the same result that came from my daughter's mother doing them to me—we're sending child support payments but there's no real or meaningful relationship with the mother or the child. Hundreds of thousands of black men deal with similar situations and, if substantial changes in child support policies and laws aren't made, hundreds of thousands more will in the near future. (The next chapter will expound more on the issue of "Payments vs. Parentage, Dollar vs. Dad.")

The second thing the black family needs from the child support system is for it to focus on enforcement of what I call "values-based parenting," not just an enforcement of finance-based parenting. This includes considering joint custody to be the true standard when it comes to parenting after divorces and split-ups. Sans abuse of some sort, this standard should never be deviated from. In my case with my daughter as well as in the 50 Cent case, joint custody should have been granted. Even Judge Judy, former family court judge and T.V. celebrity, agrees that joint custody should be the standard; she vehemently said so in a CNN interview with Larry King. "We have to be equal.... on the books, there is a law that says no one parent is favored over the other.... that's honored more in the breach than it is honored in actuality. I have been a proponent for many years of there being a presumption in this country for joint custody of children. That's where courts should start.... that should be the standard, joint custody, because children are entitled to be raised by two parents even if the parents don't get along anymore. We expect you to participate in the rearing of your children, to go to open school night, to be out there to play with them. Very often there are two people working in the household. They divide authority and you're equal except when there's a divorce. And then, how often, I ask you, do you hear it quoted in the paper 'He lost custody of his children'? You don't hear that. You hear 'She lost custody. There must be something wrong with her.' Well I think that that has to change in this country because it was my experience in the family court, and I left the family court ten years ago, but even my experience in the television courtroom suggests to me that there are as wonderful a group of fathers out there as a group of mothers and it's about time that this country recognizes that in not only the letter of the law but the spirit of the law as well."[38] I couldn't have said it better myself. If a parent arbitrarily wants to demand primary or full physical custody of a child, in the event they are granted such, that parent should be willing and able to undertake primary or full financial responsibility for that child as well. *No parent should be able to arbitrarily demand primary custody and control of a child while simultaneously demanding equal or more than equal financial contribution from the non-custodial parent.* It is an absolute shame and a travesty that joint custody is not the standard within the U.S. child support system. Maybe it's not the standard because, if heavily implemented nationally, it would negate the very need for such a robust profitable government authoritative monitoring platform that involves tens of thousands of personnel and that is used in many other illicit ways that ties into population surveillance, investigations, and big data collection from other government agencies, and some people do not want that. Hopefully, those of good will continue speaking out and making efforts seeking to change this.

But whether or not joint custody ever becomes the standard, the enforcement power of the child support system, if it must be utilized, could and should be largely redirected to enforce values-based parenting instead of finance-based parenting, which would equally require both parents to be intimately involved in the daily lives of their children in a positive way, with the potential for punitive, possibly financial consequences being levied for not doing so. If this was the mandated intent and focus of the system, we could guarantee that the general results would be better than the reality we are dealing with right now, and that statistic about nearly seventy percent of black children being raised by single mothers would at once cease to exist. Because the majority of them would be being raised by both parents, equally, no matter the status of their parent's relationship or their respective financial circumstances. As they should be. But history, which is our metaphysical teacher whom should always be listened to, tells us that, for some people who are in power in America, this would all be too much like right.

And for those within the black community who naively want to believe the child support system is their friend, despite all the glaring big-picture facts to the contrary, those two quotes at the opening of this chapter are for you. Ponder upon them. Because collectively speaking, your fake "friend" the child support system is actually your real enemy, and, by seeking and getting your complicit compliance and participation in its social scheme, is actively helping to further destabilize and destroy your community.

CHAPTER FOUR

A Flawed System
That Sets Black Children Up for Failure: Payments vs. Parentage, Dollar vs. Dad

"Don't take my baby, please don't take my baby! I've been away from my baby for two months.... I'm at thirteen thousand dollars a month, what more do you want from me?!"
– Grammy nominated singer and actor Tyrese Gibson, crying and begging his ex and the court for access to his daughter[39]

   Statistics show that for every black mother that collects child support payments in America, there is at least one black child that is growing up without their biological father being active in their daily lives.[40] So instead of all these black children's lives being prescribed by their black fathers, they are largely being prescribed by mostly conservative courts invoking rules that were designed by white politicians. And yes; many of these same courts, rules, and politicians are racist with nary a mind toward the upliftment of black families, and their acceptance of the widespread negative outcomes of their policies on the black collective openly reflects that. (Negative outcomes like multitudes of broken black families, utterly destroyed relationships, routinely incarcerated black fathers, hundreds of thousands of black men with debt they can never pay, and millions of fatherless black children. With all parties involved being monitored, studied, and controlled to an extent.) The real problem though, is how so many black people continue to play right into their hands due to widespread lack of knowledge and subconscious dependence on America's social systems to define and solve their problems for them, even though America's systems have usually *been* the source of many of black people's problems, *not* our problem solver.

Which brings to my mind a question I have often asked myself: When and why did black people begin to become so trustfully befriended to America's governmental and social systems, despite a long clear continuous history of rampant maltreatment by these same systems? As to the question of when, I guess we can go all the way back to Crispus Attucks—a mixed black and Indian man, who was the very first person to die fighting the British for American independence in the 1700's, only to have one side of his family tree wiped out and the other side enslaved for centuries in America after that. Or we can skip forward a century or two and observe the presumably heavy patriotism and faith in America's government and her systems that great blacks like the Buffalo Soldiers, the Tuskegee Airmen, Joe Louis or Martin Luther King Jr. had. I would personally argue that their hope-based faith was greatly unfounded and certainly unrewarded, which is typical, and for mainly one reason: *A manmade system is but a reflection of the men who created it, and thus in its operation can be no more just than those who created it and control it, no matter the publicly stated intent.* The long history of black people expecting justice and right treatment from systems that were created by white people is littered with examples of why that mainly hope-based expectation is almost always a mistake. And it doesn't really matter if we're talking about black people in America or black people in Europe, Africa, South America, Haiti, Jamaica, Barbados, Cuba, or anywhere else—the struggle for proper treatment from white-spawned systems of all types has remained constant from centuries back, up to this very day. History is clear and indisputable on this point.

The main issue is *why* though—why do we as a people continue trusting, believing, and faithfully hoping that our interests will be best served by systems that were set up by people that have a multi-millennial-length history of oppressing and discriminating against black people all over the globe, wherever we have coexisted? Continuing doing this is certainly not a recipe for any type of black self-reliance or power; it's a recipe that will keep future black generations just as dependent on proven hostile benefactors as their enslaved ancestors were, because they refuse to wake up and accept reality and thus not make the same types of mistakes their sullied ancestors made in this regard. It indeed seems as if too many black people simply refuse to accept reality regarding white supremacy and its apparatuses and would rather keep intuitively relying on hope and wishful thinking instead of accepting reality as it presents itself and formulating proper plans to deal with it. Today, black politicians want so badly to believe in the political systems of America; black cops want to believe in the law enforcement system of America; black judges and prosecutors and attorneys want to believe in the judicial system of America; black educators want to believe in the educational system of America; black correctional workers want to believe in the criminal justice system of America; black preachers and civil rights activists want to believe in the American Christian theological system; but the reality is that none of these systems have ever sufficiently worked to the benefit of black people nor treated black people on par with how whites are treated. *By all measures and with few exceptions, America's systems have always failed black people, continue to fail black people today, with no change to that longstanding tradition seemingly coming any time soon.* And as long as blacks are a numerical minority in this country, I, for one, expect that this will always be the case. (America's systems vs. black people will be further expounded upon in Chapter Five.) So, the question as to why many blacks seemingly still choose to regard racist American systems with a high degree of expectancy is a complex one that I don't have the answer for.

As for the system in question, the child support system, there is one main reason it does not (and will not) work in black people's best interest, and as a predictable result of this, there are several problems with the system that can be specifically identified that clearly show how the system's actions underserve the best interest of most black families, especially the children. Some of these are built-in problems that do not affect only blacks but are especially pertinent when it comes to poor blacks who are seeking court intervention for child support, as the built-in general negative results of any flawed American system are almost always naturally amplified when it deals with black people of modest means. These things together work toward constituting a vastly flawed child support system that, among other things, greatly values payments over parentage and dollars over dads:

The main reason the child support system does not (and will not) work for black families is because it was not created for black families or typical black family circumstances. The child support system was created as an affirmative action program for white women. Most people who are familiar with the subject seem to agree that there is certainly an anti-male slant within many of the child support system's policies and procedures, but I have found via research that most black people don't know *why* it's there. Well, the answer as to why the anti-male slant is there can be summed up with just four words: the American Feminist Movement. The American Feminist Movement has a lot to do with the embedded anti-male attitude of the U.S. child support system, but when it comes to the question of feminism, black women must first understand this point: the American Feminist Movement has nothing to do with you per se; it is a fight between white women and white men. The child support system was created and set up to help middle class and rich white women receive economic relief from their well-off men for the rearing of their common offspring, hence the birthing of American Feminism. It started out that way with "first wave feminism"[41] in the early 1800's—a time when nearly all black women in America were slaves—and still largely remains that way today, but many black women have seemingly become enthused about the anti-male principles within the white woman's feminist movement and thus have unwisely sought to misapply those same sentiments toward their black male counterparts. This is not warranted.

Reminiscent of the "Me Too" feminist movement that is going on right now, white women, and some sympathetic white men, started the feminist movement because white men did not treat white women as equals in any respect, by law, so they started the movement seeking more social parity between white men and white women. (The "Me Too" movement was actually initiated by a black woman but was popularized by a white woman many years after the black woman started it.[42] In other words, no one paid attention or cared when it was just the black woman pushing that agenda, which mainly is about how white men in power treat white women anyway.) White women could not vote. They could not have a will. They could not run for office or expect equal pay. They were discriminated against by their own men at every turn for a very long time, and still are, albeit to a lesser degree. *Black women were never even a part of the feminist conversation in America until black women recently made themselves a part of that conversation.* But black women in America never had the same problem with black men that white women had with white men. Black men did not control the assets of America and never have. Black men did not make the rules of American society and never have. Black women cannot say that black men have disenfranchised them and denied them their rights under the law. Black men in America have never unified in order to legislate against black women in such ways that white men have done with white women in America. The average black man in America today still, like has always been the case, either works for a white man or is duly unemployed; the average white man in America does not work for a black man and is not duly unemployed. Therefore, when black women seek to apply these feminist weapons towards black men and use the anti-male child support system against them, because it's been placed there by her kind's longstanding enemy for her to do that with, she is feeding into something that was never designed for her or her family in the first place. And as can be expected from such a thing, when all things are considered, the outcome is less than desirable to say the least.

The child support system allows emotionalism to initiate the child support process in cases yet ignores the role that negative feelings stemming from court intervention can play in creating even more hostility within families, both of which causes multiple other problems within the system. One way the child support system allows emotionalism to inject itself in the process is by not initially investigating and determining whether a child support order is even necessary, with the option to refuse judicial intervention if the child is already being sufficiently cared for by both parents. *The law should not allow for courts to be arbitrarily getting involved in family business just because one parental party is angry at the other one* (research "Malicious Mother Syndrome"). Such requests for intervention should be refused, and parents should be forced to work out their problems themselves. In cases where parents are not able to get along at all, if both parents can show that they are providing and caring for their child like any other parent would be expected to do, court intervention should not only not be required, it shouldn't be allowed. The potential for sabotage or the further poisoning of salvageable familial relationships with vitriolic feelings—because of unneeded hostile judicial intervention and the perceived unfavorable outcomes of such by parties involved—is mostly never considered by courts but it occurs all the time. Contrary to what many believe, statistics clearly show that court intervention typically helps to further break up families, not help save families,[43] and therein lies the crux of the problem.

If court intervention is requested in a case, the first goal of the child support system should be to use every means at its disposal to try to determine the truth of all relevant matters pertaining to the situation in order to find out whether the child in question in fact is or isn't being sufficiently supported and, if not, to make sure sufficient support is rendered in the future. *Support of the child would not effectively mean money only, and every situation would not require intervention.* For example, if the judge in my own child support case involving my daughter had looked at the overall situation properly and thoroughly, *with a mind not to punish me or hurt me as soon as that opportunity legally presented itself,* but to bring about a good and reasonable outcome that is based on the reality of our particular situation that is best for the child as well as myself (because our best interests as parent and child are linked indefinitely), there would probably not be so many hard feelings between my daughter's mother and myself today. Which, of course, would greatly benefit our daughter. I probably wouldn't have ever felt the need to even write this book. How could it be good for a child for their parent to be criminalized and imprisoned and/or put under life-stifling financial conditions—when there are so many better alternatives? A child support system should always be seeking out and utilizing those better alternatives, and only when it is truly necessary for the court to get involved in child parenting issues. But as it stands right now, the child support system is vastly being overused within American society, partly because of the heavy allowance of emotionalism in the process.

The child support system deliberately creates legal and permanent inequality between parents. The child support system via its anti-male policies basically splits parents into two types: an "eligible custodian" (usually the mother) and an "ineligible liable parent" (usually the father). In my opinion, child support courts deliberately making biological parents legally unequal in this way has a negative effect on the way a large proportion of families now operate, and even on how many young people today comprehend the very concept of family. Children sense this court-encouraged imbalance of parental power and it tends to affect how they treat and relate to both parents over time, especially the noncustodial parent. It is typical for the noncustodial parent to be regarded as disposable or the "spare" parent, not only by the custodial parent but also by the child, as a result of sensing that imbalance within the family situation. The custodial parent for all intents and purposes is considered the "main" parent. This sort of parental arrangement shouldn't exist nor be promoted by the courts under the normal circumstances, and to my knowledge there has never been any stated justification given as to why the laws that govern child support choose to make parents legally unequal in this way. Some differences can and do occur when it comes to defining the roles of each parent when caring for their children, but those different roles should be formulated and agreed to by the parents, not imagined, invoked, and mandated by standardized governmental laws and policies without proper justification.

Ironically, in many if not most cases, courts don't even bother to take proper account of the time children spend with the liable parent or promote shared parenting,[44] thus it would be hard for the average liable parent to reach the legal threshold of time spent with the child that is necessary to lower or negate child support payments under most custody agreements. So, when it comes to black parenting specifically, there are already more than enough societal and economic roadblocks that set the odds against many black parents who are trying to raise their offspring together in a fashion that is wholesome and healthy; family courts do not need to be reinforcing that existing hardship by creating legal inequality between black parents. Contrarily, if there is one group of children in America who need specific policies aimed at keeping their fathers equally involved in their lives and *not* policies that disempower, undervalue, and incarcerate their fathers, it's black children.

The child support system helped create the "Bitter Baby Mama" syndrome and "Deadbeat Dad" racist stereotype in the black community. Both of these false narratives have been used to further stereotype black mothers as well as black fathers. The deadbeat dad myth was actually spawned by a CBS News report that was aired in 1986 titled, *The Vanishing Family: A Crisis in Black America*.[45] That biased and racist report featured, among other things, a somewhat disturbed black man from New Jersey who was boasting about not providing financial child support for his six children. The story (I call it a pretext for anti-black legislation) sparked immediate bombastic outrage all across the country and subsequently played a major role in state and federal legislators of both political parties then passing much stricter child support laws—as if the so-called "deadbeat" disturbed guy in that news report represented the normal rule, not the abnormal exception to the rule, in the black community. Not long after that feature was aired on TV, Congress passed several punitive laws that forced states to pursue child support debts much more aggressively.[46] (Doesn't the fact that this happened amount to blockbuster evidence as to who punitive child support laws are actually aimed at?) As a result, this has helped create a new stereotype that has transcended into labeling black men who ever have trouble paying their child support as "deadbeat dads."

In America, white men are typically not used or seen as the face of the "deadbeat dad" misnomer, despite the fact that *the child support system was first created to impel white men to take care of their children*.[47] The same way white males are not seen as the face of vices like pimping or drug dealing in America, despite white men being the creators and originators and main benefactors of such vices in this country, at the highest levels. Certain negative group attributes and personal behaviors that are in actuality shared by all races of people in America always seem to somehow get stereotypically applied only to black people, no matter the facts. When it comes to the notion of deadbeat dads, white men were the original deadbeat dads, and not just with regard to their white offspring—also with regard to their multitudes of black offspring by enslaved black women, which they almost never took care of or claimed and often sold as property. (Which mainly accounts for most blacks in the Americas and the Caribbean today being of a much lighter skin hue than their enslaved ancestors).

The "bitter baby mama" label is another example of anti-black racist stereotyping. We've all heard the cliché about how hell hath no fury like "a woman scorned"—but I don't recall ever hearing about it applying only to one particular race of women. When it comes to feminine anger or vengeful emotional reactions that can arise as it relates to a broken relationship, I personally do not know whether or not there are any real tangible or intangible differences between women of different races, but I do know this: black women are put forth as the face of the "bitter baby mama" stereotype. I believe this to be partly due to racial bias and stereotyping, since it's likely that women of all races do the exact same things that define the stereotype. But I also believe that certain aspects of the stereotype have developed into a very real common syndrome within the psyche of many black women in America. To my recollection, the very terms "baby mama" and "baby daddy" were created by black folk for black folk, and right along with those two terms was usually an underlying notion of an expectation of an adversarial relationship. In other words, "baby mamas" are typically not on the best of terms with the "baby daddy," or at least not in a stable one-household relationship together. The two terms seem to have been created with these very negative connotations built into them. I blame the child support system for helping to spawn this widespread psychologically divisive train of thought and for giving legs to it, because the result of the processes the system has in place is that most black children today are being raised by a "baby mama" who is perpetually at odds with "baby daddy," with the courts playing the divisive middle man that values payments over parentage and dollars over dads, making it worse in the long term for all parties involved.

Apart from single mothers who have no choice but to put the fathers of their children on court-ordered child support, I believe many black women today just don't have a proper understanding of how they are hurting their families by needlessly involving the government in their family business, and thus haven't considered alternatives to court intervention. While others do not care about any of that because they are angry and want to get back at "baby daddy" for some reason and are willing to use the antagonistic anti-black anti-male court system to do it, like was the case with my daughter's mother. I am writing this book for the awareness benefit of the first type of mother I just described, not the second type, because vengeful scorned people tend not to care about the big picture scenario or what makes sense. Still, despite the fact that women of all races do many of these same things and act in these same ways albeit often within a different historical and familial context, the negative stereotype and label of being a "bitter baby mama" is typically not applied to them.

The child support system places a higher value on a dollar than a dad. The system basically tells men that they do not have to be actual parents as long as they pay an amount of money that is calculated by the court, through the court. High priority is placed solely on the financial aspect of child support, and the parental aspect, which involves time spent, often gets ignored by family courts. As previously stated, family courts tend not to even take proper account of the time a child in question spends with their liable parent[48] (usually the father) and mothers are rarely ever punished for purposefully keeping children away from their fathers[49] (something that happens all too often). On the flip side of that, I've seen many fathers that actually spend more time with their children than the mothers still be made to pay full child support. Mothers certainly aren't ever threatened with imprisonment for being poor or out of work, but fathers are routinely threatened with imprisonment for being poor and/or out of work. Black men have consistently had an unemployment rate that's double or triple that of white men;[50] which inevitably means that black men will be pursued and punished more by the child support system for being unemployed, underemployed, or otherwise financially disabled. Yet there are absolutely no punitive consequences for fathers not spending time with their offspring. Black men are sent to prison for up to five years for "felony nonsupport of a dependent" all the time,[51] but I have never heard of one case where "nonsupport" was defined by anything other than money.

The child support system typically puts little to no binding requirements on custodial parents to make long-term financial contributions toward the child, and the custodian has no accountability to spend the child support money on the child. Unlike noncustodial parents, custodial parents aren't made/expected to earn money through paid work so that the standard of living of their child is improved, or so that the financial burden on the liable parent can be reduced whenever applicable. Many custodial parents can and do work once their kids are in school or if they have available child care or when they get with a new partner, but under the current system there's no direct incentive or stated requirement for them to work, and there should be. A liable parent is forced to work and pay full *and visible* child support for eighteen years or more, while the custodial parent is not forced to do anything but is *assumed* to make a commensurate financial effort toward the child's wellbeing. When custodial parents do work, they can generally earn as much money as they like and this does not bring them into court scrutiny or even affect the amount of money that the liable parent must pay. Whenever the custodial parent doesn't work and/or has received welfare, the courts still take into account the finances of the noncustodial parent but mostly for the system's benefit, not the child's benefit. Because if the custodial parent receives child support payments and is or has been on welfare, the government will seek to reduce the amount of welfare benefits received based on that, as well as recoup past welfare payments made to the custodial parent from the liable parent. *Welfare benefits received by custodial parents have to be paid back to the government by noncustodial parents, not by the custodial parents who actually received the benefits.* This is not fair, to say the least. And even with regard to those received welfare benefits that noncustodial parents (like myself) have to pay back to the government, the custodial parents are not technically required to spend it on the child but are not given nearly the same wide-ranging spending leeway they are given with child support money that comes from liable parents. Also, If the custodian happens to get a new partner who brings extra income into the household, child support payments are theoretically supposed to be adjusted and welfare benefits stopped, but rarely are.

So why is there no accountability whatsoever on how received child support funds get spent? If you're getting food stamps, there are in-place restrictions on how those can be spent. You cannot use food stamps to buy a car or buy clothes. You cannot even purchase a hot food plate with food stamps. If you get a loan for a house or a car, you must spend the money on a house or a car. But there is absolutely no regulation on how child support funds are utilized by custodial parents! The custodian gets to spend the child support money they receive however they see fit. There is no binding obligation to spend it on the child or to prove to anyone that it was done (least of all to the liable parent). Also, because the child support system typically doesn't differentiate between amounts of money paid and the actual real costs of rearing the child, the accountability of the custodian to spend the child support funds on the child is even further reduced. This is highly problematic, yet is one of the easiest fixes out of everything that's wrong with the system. *If courts demanded line item accountability with regard to how child support funds get spent, with real repercussions for any improper action, that alone would eliminate much of what is wrong with the child support system.* (In the rare cases where some states have made custodial parents financially accountable to spend the child support money on the child, the child usually ends up with nothing and the custodian still gets a slap on the wrist.[52]) Monies paid for the maintenance of a child should only be spent on the maintenance of that child and nothing else. And custodial parents should have to show and prove that they did so, to the courts as well as to the liable parent who paid the money.

For noncustodial parents of means, the amount paid is often not based on the true cost of supporting the child. In all child support cases, the *actual* cost of supporting the children should be tabulated and the amount of money paid should always be reflective of that cost. However, for no apparent reason, the government instead decided to base the amount of payments on the liable parent's "capacity to pay." It is almost subjective to clearly determine what one's "capacity to pay" actually is, whereas the actual cost of supporting a child is usually self-evident. But the government takes it upon itself to decide for parents what is or is not a reasonable amount of money for supporting a child, and this practice has been most problematic and unfair for both poor noncustodial parents as well as those who are financially stable. In cases where the noncustodial parent happens to be financially well-off, the often-used legal argument for this is that "a child needs to live a lifestyle that is similar to the parent of means," but that argument is greatly undermined by the fact that there is absolutely no enforcement or supervision on how those funds are appropriated or spent once surrendered, and the parent of means, if the father, is not typically considered for full custody, so that he may most directly provide that high lifestyle the child is "entitled" to. So, regardless of huge amounts of money being sent in many cases, there is still no guarantee that it is exclusively benefiting the child. Court-ordered child support is not supposed to be a form of alimony or ex-partner support, and should not be allowed to be spent as if it were.

Also, there is no reason why both separated parents should not have the same finance-based parental rights as parents who are married to one another or otherwise co-parenting in their own way. A non-custodial parent shouldn't be disallowed the same choice-making abilities that all other parents are allowed, when it comes to their child and money. Every parent who has natural custody of their child can decide for themselves what clothes to buy that child, what foods to feed the child, what lifestyle the child will live. Some parents choose to pay for their children's college education, while other parents require their children to get either a scholarship or a job to pay for it. One of the richest men in the world, Warren Buffett, has publicly stated that he will not be leaving his multi-billion-dollar estate to his offspring,[53] and it is his right to make that choice. If Buffett, who was married to their mother until her death, had elected not to raise them as "rich kids," that would also have been his choice and his parental right, as some rich parents elect not to spend a lot of money on their children. These are the natural choice-rights of all parents, but the child support system completely strips noncustodial parents of these types of parental choice-rights while simultaneously placing very unreasonable and unfair financial burdens on many noncustodial parents.

As a result of all these things I've pointed out, there are two things that are absolutely for certain about the child support system where black people are concerned: the system was not initially meant for us, and the system is not currently working for us. It's not working for rich black people and it certainly is not working for poor black people. Usually things that aren't meant for you will not work well for you; you will either have to find a way to transform it so that it may also work for you, in your best interest, or leave it alone. These have always been the two choices for black people in America when it comes to dealing with such social systems that were not created by us or for us but that we nevertheless must eventually participate in, endure, and seek to overcome. Most of the real casualties of the child support system go unseen and unheard of, as many experiences of poor black people do, because no one really cares about what happens to poor black people in this country. Politicians don't even talk about the poor at all, not even poor whites; only the middle class and the rich. So, when poor people of any background get caught up in social systems like the child support system, that were fashioned by and for middle class and rich white people, they are likely to be mishandled. And if those poor people happen to be black as well, mishandled even more so.

CHAPTER FIVE

Another Form of Probation, Parole, & Control for Black Men: Why Punitive Child Support Enforcement Procedures & Penalties Tend to Affect Black Fathers Differently & Disproportionately

> "And why half of my whole hood on papers
> Some are on house arrest,
> some are on child support,
> Some of 'em did they bid,
> the other half waiting to go to court"
> – Rapper Plies
> on song "Welcome to My Hood"[54]

Many black people, again, because of that ever-present false hope that the largess of whites will suddenly stop seeking to do the sort of racist and exclusionary things they have always done with regard to us wherever we have coexisted in the world (i.e. slavery, colonialism, Jim Crow, apartheid, segregation, institutionalizing racism, redlining, etc.), evidently fail to realize that many of the easily discernable overtly racist systems, practices, and apparatuses of the past, and the purposes thereof, didn't just suddenly disappear or become obsolete; they simply evolved and modernized. They evolved and modernized into much more sophisticated versions of themselves that are purposely made harder to see and label as what they really are and for what they really do, as far as black people are concerned. Liberal concepts of modernization and political correctness are now applied to just about everything, so that everything, including social systems, at least has the surface appearance of operating from the principles of fairness and equality. However, the essence of what they are about when it comes to black people never really changes despite appearing to do so on the surface, and they almost never can withstand up-close analysis and observation without being revealed to be what they were and still are—anti-black.

The easiest way to detect what these sorts of systems are and what their true intentions are is to closely analyze the results they bring about within society and then observe and analyze the attitude of acceptability or unacceptability of those results that's subsequently shown by the creators of those systems. If the results and outcomes of any particular legislative or social ventures are shown to be largely negative and racist and proven to mainly hurt black people, but it's not quickly done away with or revised, then it can rightly be concluded that said result was likely a part of the intended purpose, whether openly stated or not. This is how we know the plantation system of America evolved into a robust prison system, and why. This is how we know slavery evolved into Jim Crow and then into a racist hierarchal worker system that keeps most blacks on the bottom. This is how we know why the various dishonest peace treaties that multiple generations of this nation's powerful elite made with the Indian tribes evolved into Indian reservations — because it was *always* the underlying intent of the American government to take all their land for itself. Just as it has *always* been the expressed and unexpressed intent of many whites in this country to hurt and undermine black people wherever and however they can, and history does not permit any disputation of this as fact. It is no wonder then, and should not come as a surprise to anyone that, regarding child support debt and black men, *the way that "systematically created" debt was used to incarcerate and to oppress black men during the Reconstruction and Jim Crow eras with racist peonage, convict, and sharecropping debt calculative techniques,*[55] *child support debt is being used in the exact same way with the exact same effect.*

The first book I wrote ten years ago, *Why Are So Many Black Men in Prison?,* was the very first book ever written that thoroughly exposed the prison system in America, which is often rightly called The American Prison Industrial Complex, as corrupt, racist, and nothing more than a modernized for-profit form of plantation neo-slavery. In the book, I explained and showed how deliberately the U.S. prison system has been hijacked and commissioned to serve as a stifling entity in the lives of black people, particularly black males, seeking to heavily criminalize and incarcerate a massive number of black males and stem black population growth at the same time. Since that book's publication, many more concurring books have been written on the subject (most notably Michelle Alexander's bestselling book *The New Jim Crow*, which I personally consider to be a corporatized copycat version of my book, right down to the cover). As a result, it has now been all but admitted by our government that well-used dog whistle politicized terms like "War on Drugs" were nothing but white/right-wing political schemes meant to primarily target, stifle, and hurt black people. Many white so-called liberals like former president Bill Clinton—whom many blacks lovingly dubbed "the first black president" before Obama—went right along with these schemes and many times even spearheaded such efforts.[56] Then, years later, after the damage has been done and the predictable negative effects of that effort have been exposed, they will often openly admit their "mistakes" in supporting those particular schemes yet still will go on to support newer updated political and legislative schemes of the same sort that have the same type of negative affect on the black community. This sort of game is played on black people all the time, yet many blacks continue to find reason to have faith in America's politicians and social systems, and that they will at some point serve their best interest.

A Form of Probation, Parole, and Control for Black Men | 89

I pointed out in that book that, on any given day, there are a million or more black males locked up in jails or prisons in America, with several million more that are on probation or parole.[57] Those are astounding numbers. Nearly one third of all black men in America have spent some time in jail or have been on probation or parole or house arrest.[58] Statistics show that black men are more likely to spend time in jail or prison than any other male racial group.[59] And most black men in prison have at least one child.[60] Add to that equation the fact that many of these incarcerated men are poor[61] and the women they have children with are likely to be poor as well and likely to have received welfare benefits at one time or another during the child's life. Which means that once they are released, these men will have mandatory child support debts that will have been placed on them that will likely never get paid off. The average prison stint for black men in America is over ten years,[62] which means that a man who serves ten years in jail and who has just one child would, if placed on child support, be hit with an interest-accrued debt of around $30,000 upon his release. Which means that, once released from prison, these fathers will likely always be under the scrutiny and threat of a judge reincarcerating them if said judge should decide to do so. In cases where the mother was not on public assistance, she can still demand that same amount of back pay for the years the father was incarcerated, which happens all of the time, and such demands are never refused by the courts. If there is one thing that I can personally vouch for, it's that being under constant threat of incarceration is no way to live, especially for a formerly incarcerated person, and certainly isn't a viable way to encourage responsible parental involvement and/or family cohesion from a judicial bully pulpit. There's no wonder why over eighty percent of all black men who are released from prison are re-arrested within just five years of release;[63] among many other reasons, the main reason is that nobody wants to give them a real chance at even survival, let alone success. In this regard, the child support system is no different.

About thirty percent of the families currently in the child support system are living below the federal poverty line,[64] which means the "enforcement" aspect of the child support system—which is about collecting monies by way of threats, crippling sanctions, and incarceration—typically comes into play when dealing with the poorest of American families and fathers, many of whom are, of course, black men.[65] And since most of those who are on court-ordered child support are men, let's deal with it from a male perspective. The racial wage gap shows that white men in America get paid an average of $21 an hour while black men get paid an average of $15 an hour, and the wage gap has not changed on paper in nearly forty years.[66] And I specify "on paper" because in actuality the "wage" gap between black men and white men is much wider than this plain jane statistic suggests. In the real world, when you factor in tangible things like ownership of industries and large corporations and land and who ultimately has control of most of the wealth, resources, networks, and power apparatuses of America, there is generally no real comparison between what the average white man has and earns and has access to and what the average black man has and earns and has access to.

In fact, probably upwards of ninety percent of all black male workers in America work for white male-owned companies and institutions (including state governments and the federal government), while comparably few white men work for companies owned by black men. I would even go as far as to say that there are probably very few cities and towns in America where you can count the number of white males who work for black-owned companies with your fingers and need more than one hand, if any. But I seriously doubt anyone could find even a single black neighborhood anywhere in America where you can count the black males who work for white males or other nonblacks on just one hand; you will likely need all of your fingers and toes and the fingers and toes of many others to count them. The ownership class in America is now and always has been nearly exclusively white—white and male, to be exact. Therefore, it goes without saying that most white males, even working-class white males, would not have serious problems when it comes to being able to pay court-ordered child support because most white males don't have a serious problem finding gainful employment (from other white males) and making sufficient money. As pointed out in chapter one, studies have indeed shown that a white male ex-con with only a high school diploma can have an equal or better chance of getting a job, from a member of his own race, than a black male college graduate who has no criminal record.

Unfortunately, and conveniently for the government, child support data isn't currently collected or analyzed by race, and it should be. This is something else that needs to be changed. However, there are certain things we can still discern about the race factor from the data that is put forth. Given black men's longstanding well-documented disadvantages in American society and its workplaces, it's safe to presume that black men disproportionately owe child support debt, and not mainly because they are "deadbeats" or inherently negligent or lazy, as new-age racist stereotypes hope to suggest. (Current Speaker of the House Paul Ryan has gone on record saying that the problem with "inner city" men is that they are lazy and are "not even thinking about working or learning the value and the culture of work."[67]) While research actually suggests that most black fathers want to support their children,[68] research also suggests that financial strain all too often causes and sustains family dissolution.[69] Studies and research also show that at least two-thirds of all unpaid court-ordered child support comes from a periodic recurring inability to pay, not a lack of desire to support one's children.[70] Therefore, in situations where poor black families face strained or broken relationships and children are involved, the typical response should not be to run to the court system to get it involved. Because the truth is, though somewhat quietly, this misapplied and overused practice of requesting court involvement in family situations has been slowly devastating the black community.

The reality is, most of the black men who are in the child support system are nowhere near what you would call "financially stable,"[71] and this fact, more so than any other fact, is the direct reason why the child support system acts as more of an oppressive entity for black men who are in it than it does for others. "Twenty percent of the people in the (child support) system shouldn't be in there because they're too poor," says David J. Pate, an associate professor of social work at the University of Wisconsin, Milwaukee. "Those $10,000 or even $20,000 earners."[72] The U.S. government, according to Pate, is owed over 115 billion dollars in child support, but seventy percent of that money is owed by Americans who make less than $10,000 a year.[73] In other words, it is pretty safe to say that this is money that primarily *black fathers* owe to the government. I want us to please pause for a minute here and let the ridiculousness and magnitude of that reality sink in, because this is yet more blockbuster evidence that the child support system is a grand failure and an oppressive, suppressive force on the black community.

In all likelihood, black men owe to the U.S. government, in interest-accruing child support debt and associated fees, about a third of what the U.S. government spends annually on welfare benefits for black women. The U.S. government spends around 750 billion dollars per year on welfare benefits, and black women are about forty percent of all U.S. welfare recipients.[74] That amounts to roughly about 300 million dollars that poor black women receive in annual assistance from the government. This is at a time when more black women are graduating college than black men and can earn as much as black men in the workplace.[75] So why are these poor men, who also have children that they are financially responsible for supporting, generally not afforded this same level of government assistance? Why is the male typically denied welfare benefits, despite him being just as poor and still having to provide for his children via child support? Why is there a difference made between a poor woman with children and a poor man with children, in this day and age? Is it not unfair that, while under the exact same life circumstances, one gender gets government assistance with no debt, while the other gender gets government debt with no assistance? During my research for this book, I found that there are multitudes of everyday black men who have child support debts that are upward of $100,000—many of them being that high of an amount partly due to heavy interest being applied plus multiple "processing fees"—whom have never earned over $25,000 in a year in their entire lives.

I also found out during my research that most people don't even know that child support debt accrues between four and twelve percent interest, annually.[76] And why should money that is owed for child support even accrue interest? This isn't money that technically could've been used by the custodial parent for personal investments or put into an interest-accumulating fund or something, which is the usual argument for applying interest in legal situations where monies are owed to someone. This is money that, if sent on time, is only supposed to be used toward the welfare of the child for that month. Not saved. Not invested. Not spent on anything else. So, what is the real purpose and effect of high compound interest being placed on child support debt that is owed to the government by mostly poor men? Just how are they supposed to ever pay such debt? With such laws and policies in place, these men will likely never get to enjoy the basic human freedom and dignity that other citizens enjoy because it is largely denied them due to the heavy scrutiny that comes with owing those kinds of debts to a government agency, or having debt enforced by a government agency.

Whenever there is a civil judgement rendered against a defendant in civil court, that debt judgement is not subsequently enforced by the state; the plaintiff has the onus to seek and find out how to collect what they are owed. But when it comes to child support, supposedly "for the sake of the child," the state and the federal government take on the burden of enforcing debt judgements if the custodial parent initiates the process. Only in such cases where the custodial parent has received welfare benefits and the father is verified, will the state initiate debt collection on its own, with the tacit consent of the custodial parent. In most child support cases that I'm familiar with, the court almost always has the full consent of the custodial parent to go after the non-custodial parent, because there are ways around letting the system get involved, even with one having been on welfare. So, if a custodial parent really did not want the other parent to be placed under the strict scrutiny of the child support system and wanted to keep their family business internal, there are ways that she or he could prevent that from happening. There are indeed many black women who choose to go this route, but they are seemingly the exceptions to the rule. The government, through the child support system, has made it far too appealing and easy for parents and families to become dependent on it and to abandon the notion, almost totally, of working out their own issues.

Including incarceration in the lengthy list of allowable punishments for late or missed child support payments, at the supposed behest of the child's best interest, is one of the more rancid policies of the child support system. Locking up a child's parent over money is synonymous to telling that child that you are helping him or her by crippling and torturing one of their two parents. And I'll be the first to tell you, from experience: imprisonment IS torture! In more ways than I can count. Even if it's for just one day. And not just for the one being imprisoned; it is also torture for that person's family, including the child over which the parent is being jailed. It is torture for that person's parents, for their spouse or current partner, for their other offspring if they have any, and for anyone else that loves that person. When a man is locked up for child support debt, he will be housed with the murderers and killers and rapists and gangbangers and will potentially be exposed to all kinds of jailhouse nastiness and savagery during his stay. Prisons and jails should only be for people who have committed serious criminal activity in society, not people who are in government-created debt to their own child's other parent.

Data shows that most men who are ever incarcerated for child support are jobless or severely underemployed at the time,[77] which makes it even more ridiculous that the system still sees fit to incarcerate them despite those circumstances. Men who have gainful employment are almost never incarcerated over child support debt, which again proves that most men have no problem with paying child support for their children and would almost always choose to pay money over being incarcerated, no matter the amount requested. To me, it's common sense that a man who allows himself to be jailed, even for one day, over child support money doesn't have the money necessary to prevent it from happening. Again, which is why working men are not typically jailed for child support. But I have personally observed the child support system effectively seek to extort money from noncustodial parents—even from family members and friends of men who are under threat of incarceration for missed or late payments or back pay, just because they do not want to see that man go to jail. The same way the prison system basically extorts huge sums of money from the families of thousands of black men and women who get incarcerated in America on any given day, in exchange for grossly overpriced goods and services like phone calls and toiletries. That is because both systems, the child support system and the prison system, are two different teeth in the mouth of the same monster. And neither system cares about where the money comes from—there are multitudes of black men who sell drugs and even rob and steal to, among other things, pay child support. I have never heard of a case where any scrutiny or criticism is given by the system for doing that, or any concern or assistance being offered to someone who feels they must commit crimes to get money to keep up with child support payments and thus stay out of jail. Risking jail to stay out of jail, is what it amounts to, and trust me, there are thousands of disenfranchised black men who are engaged in this. Then, when they finally get caught for the criminal activity, it's a double whammy because now they are not only in trouble for that, they will also be "criminally" in debt and subject to future reincarceration for child support back pay, once they get out of jail.

Due to the inherent unfairness in the system, there are also many black men who have been financially well-off in the past, but for whatever reason aren't anymore, who are under threat of incarceration but who have already paid the mother of their children more money than she has ever earned on her own in her entire life. Many of these men have paid more money in a single year to a woman, for one child, than most parents would spend to raise five children, college expenses included. For many black entertainers and especially black athletes, this is especially problematic since most of them are broke or bankrupt within three years of retiring from their sport or livelihood.[78] The internet is full of heinous stories like this. Sean Levert, the youngest son of Rock & Roll Hall of Famer O'Jay's singer Eddie Levert, died in jail after being sentenced to serve twenty-two months for inability to pay nearly $90,000 in back child support.[79] New Orleans rapper Juvenile was arrested and got sentenced to thirty days in lockup in 2017 for owing $150,000 for payments missed during 2012 and 2013 to a woman for one child, just two months after he had given her $20,000 in cash in court.[80] Legendary Boxer Zab Judah was arrested in 2017 and sentenced to three months for owing over $120,000 in "calculated" child support.[81] Each of these three men, over the time of the respective children's lives, allegedly had already given those mothers of their children more money than would be required to sufficiently raise multiple children. Mike Epps, the famous comedian, was recently ordered to pay his ex-wife $15,000 per month in just child support,[82]—which doesn't even include nearly $100,000 annually for hair care expenses, private school and medical, on top of $25,000 monthly in spousal support— and the payments won't end unless she remarries (which we all know she likely will not do, unless it is to a richer man). Each year, Epps will spend about $275,000 on "child support" alone, but we all know that it is really just auxiliary ex-wife support. It will likely not be mostly spent on the children; as some of the richest men in the world who are married with kids don't spend that kind of money every year on their children. Yet history shows that many of these types of women are very likely to support and even request the incarceration of their child's father should he ever have financial problems and those gigantic child support payments slow down or stop. The fact that he's already paid enough to raise the child ten times over will mean absolutely nothing to them, or to the court.

Regardless of the income levels involved, jailing parents for child support debt is almost never a good thing. Not from the children in question's perspective, and not from the taxpayer's perspective. It does not help the situation in any way, nor has it ever been proven to be a necessary element of good child support enforcement. People are not jailed for unpaid civil judgements, student loans, or even unpaid bills, which are all legitimate and legally enforceable debts. The main two debts that can send you to jail today are tax debt and child support debt. The Fair

Debt and Collection Practice Act even prohibits debt collectors from threatening people with criminal prosecution for failing to pay debts, *unless* those debts are due to either taxes or child support. Because the practice of incarcerating parents over missed child support payments has never been proven or shown to be a needed part of child support enforcement, no one really knows exactly why child support debt was included within this sparse detainable debt category.

Child support debt accounts are also placed on credit reports, which means that men who have back pay debts or missed payments are sure to have bad credit scores, and again, no government official has ever given a public explanation as to why this is being done or just how this practice benefits the overall situation. The average credit score for black men is generally much lower than that of white men,[83] and I would submit that massive child support debt, among many other factors of course, has a lot to do with that. When your earnings are low and your debts are very high, that scenario tends to cause a person more problems than those who have higher earnings, on credit reports. And when you are black and male with a bad credit score, you tend to have nothing coming and/or will be severely upcharged even more so than others, and that's if you ever are able to use your credit to purchase something. (The credit system, like the child support system and many other government systems, has not served black people well. Nor was it ever intended or likely to do so. But that's another subject for another chapter, which happens to be the next chapter.)

So, while both rich men and poor men alike, albeit for different reasons, all of which are unfair, can at certain points face incarceration for child support, the system eats the poor more readily, and unlike the stories I just recounted about several celebrities, their horror stories go largely untold. The poor and the disenfranchised are mainly the ones who are going through prison and jail doors over child support, and it's usually a revolving door for them. And that's exactly how the system is set up to work. For example, in Memphis, Tennessee where I live, if a child support defendant is unemployed or has no discernible income at the particular time the child support case is heard, an income amount is arbitrarily attributed to the defendant by the state and the support payments are then calculated from that *because it is assumed that the person can obtain employment that will provide them around that amount of income.* In Tennessee, that amount is about $36,370.00 for male parents and $26,990.00 for female parents.[84] Yet, known racial disparities in income are not factored into these equations. The average annual income for a black household in Memphis, that's headed by both a man and a woman, is around $30,300,[85] which is much lower than the superficial $36,370 figure that is used in child support court and attributed just to the non-custodial parent. Whereas the average income for a white male-headed household in Memphis is markedly higher;

around $54,000.[86] Blacks in Memphis make up seventy-five percent of all families making under $10,000 a year, despite being the majority population of the city, while whites make up eighty-one percent of all the households making more than $200,000 a year in Memphis.[87] Thus, it goes without saying that the system's whole approach is wrongheaded and needs changing. Poor men should not be being punished essentially for being poor.

I have never heard of anyone ever suggesting that poor mothers be put in jail for not being able to adequately take care of a child financially, and it's obviously because everyone seems to understand that the child still needs its mother regardless. But evidently the system does not feel that fathers are really needed, therefore it has no problem with locking the father up for essentially being poor or financially distressed. If a mother falls on hard times, she is not in peril of being sent to prison for that. But if a father falls on hard times, he can be sent to prison. Even if a woman states that she does not know who the father of her child is, she will still be eligible to receive state benefits and will never be required to reimburse the state for those benefits. But if the father of that child is known, *he will automatically be held responsible for a "debt" to the state, even if he himself is indigent and/or in need of welfare benefits*. Why are poor fathers forced to repay the government for welfare assistance received by the mother, but mothers are never forced to pay it back under any circumstances? Not even those mothers who don't know the identities of the fathers of their children or whose children's fathers are dead, disabled, or in prison are forced to repay the government for welfare benefits they received—so what is the point of making a difference in consequences between the male and female in this scenario, and what is the real purpose of such an asinine practice? Why are poor men ignored and treated so differently than poor women in these circumstances? Why is her "poorness" forgiven by the government but his is not? These are all very valid questions that demand an answer.

One of the most negatively effective tools the child support system uses in its persecutory pursuit to criminalize and incarcerate black fathers is its rank policy of making outrageous, unreasonable lump sum payment demands and extortions upon them, usually at the request of the custodial parent, whereby the judge demands a payment of several months or even several years back pay all at once, with immediate incarceration as the penalty for not being able to make the large payment on the spot. The average working person in America has less than $1,000 in savings;[88] hardly anyone can be asked to produce large amounts of money on the spot and be expected to have it, but the system has no problem making such demands on unemployed and disenfranchised destitutes and even ex-prisoners, who virtually have no real chance at securing gainful employment in America. This policy is just one more makes-no-sense invention of someone's deranged mind, and most times only leads to the obvious outcome; another black man entering into the prison system, and for no good reason. For inflated debt that in all likelihood he will never get fully paid off. Which, if you ask me, is the designed intent and purpose of any system that would much rather incarcerate black fathers in need rather than help black fathers in need. Ours is a system that openly encourages the dissolution and breakup of black families with its policies. It is a system that allows for rampant abuse and overuse at the expense of family cohesion and against the basic interests of black children, which all comes at the expense of taxpayers, who have to foot most of the bill whenever a poor person is incarcerated. It is a system that literally encourages parents to abandon the notion of working their issues out together out-of-court in favor of them becoming virtual adversaries that routinely and angrily seek each other's destruction within a courtroom setting, for the supposed sake of children they happily laid down and created together outside of the courtroom. The corrupt child support system, aided by many of us who really should know better, is perfectly and purposely designed to oblige, host, and assist in all such destructive efforts.

Until January 2017, most states actually legally defined an incarcerated father as "voluntarily unemployed," not involuntarily unemployed,[89] as if the incarcerated father made a choice to be in jail and thus not employed. Which meant that, since black men are three times as likely to be incarcerated in America when compared to men of other races,[90] they were more likely to accrue even larger child support debt while incarcerated that would be like a ball and chain on their lives for many years, if not their entire lives. President Barack Obama, via a "midnight" regulations revision in his last month in office, quietly brought an end to this egregious longstanding practice of courts considering incarcerated fathers to be voluntarily unemployed, though as I'm writing this book it is not clear if President Trump will allow it to remain the law long-term.[91] In my opinion, President Obama should have done it much earlier, but he obviously knew it wouldn't be liked by conservative whites and that he would face a backlash. For this same reason, many of the few things Obama did that positively affected the black condition were done in his last term toward the end of term.[92]

And since out of wedlock births are higher for blacks, as mentioned before, this also means more black men are being placed on court-ordered child support and under threat of imprisonment for financial reasons. But as I have stated, real child "support" is not only financial and the focus should be as much or more about the parental participation in the child's life. If a non-custodial parent has to go to jail over perceived parental deficiencies or inadequacies, I personally would rather that parent go to jail for something like missing their child's graduation ceremony or not spending any time with their child, as opposed to going for some missed payments, especially if the child in question isn't starving or unduly suffering due to lack of financial support. No parent should be able to just walk away from their parental responsibilities without penalty, but common sense and a desire for fair outcomes that work toward the common good of society have to be infused into the process of ensuring parental responsibility in situations where parents just cannot see eye to eye or work together. Laws and policies should be formulated and enacted to encourage that to happen, not discourage it. And incarceration of a parent should never be on the table except for rare mitigating circumstances involving rank parental negligence.

With all that being said, let me say this: I understand that many black single mothers have it really hard, and I, for one, am certainly pro-black, pro-family, and pro-black woman. Every book I have written thus far is pertaining to the wellbeing of black people—it is a subject I am fully dedicated to. In my second book, *Getting Out & Staying Out: A Black Man's Guide to Success After Prison*, which was a success guide for black male ex-prisoners about what to do once they get released, I dedicated an entire chapter to urging post-prison black men to settle down, preferably with a woman of color, to do right by her and treat her like a queen, and to work toward entrepreneurship and progress with her. I come from a family full of single black women with children and women who have their children's fathers on child support. My own mother had my dad on child support. So, I get it. I'm fully aware that single black women who work earn less than any other working demographic in America.[93] I'm aware that half of American households with children under the age of eighteen include a mother who is either the primary or sole earner for her family.[94] (This is due to many things, including lower marriage rates and higher divorce rates.) So, I understand that for unemployed or lower wage earning single black women with children especially, the need for support from the father is day to day and it is very real. And there certainly are men who have to be forced to provide support for their children. However, I believe, as the evidence suggests, that those type of men are exceptions to the rule and not the rule. The U.S. child support system has evolved to be as robust as it is because federal and state governments choose to promote the irresponsible and false narrative that most fathers, especially black fathers, are inherently "bad," as well as the subsequent over-reliance on the system by millions of mothers and ex-wives, many of whom have unrighteous motivations that are rooted in anger and personal revenge. The result is an unbalanced system that treats fathers as unequal parents and acts as if the best or only thing fathers can do for their children is provide money.

The purpose of this book is to make everyone aware that there are very serious flaws within the current child support system that, when you look at the big picture, are having a more harmful rather than helpful effect within our community. Overall, what I am proposing and what I would like to see changed with regard to the system is: more joint custody rulings rendered; fewer child support cases undertaken by the courts; more scrutiny of how child support payments are spent; incarceration taken off the list of common penalties for child support debt; and, as far as the black community is concerned, less reliance on the child support system—at least until the issues outlined in this book are dealt with.

CHAPTER SIX

Beware of "The Systems"

> "You're living in poverty. Your schools are no good. You have no jobs. Fifty-eight percent of your youth is unemployed. What the hell do you have to lose?"
> Donald Trump, speaking to black people, 2016[95]

When Donald Trump made the above statement on the campaign trail, it was one of the few statements that he ever made as a presidential candidate that absolutely no one in the media said was untrue. Lots of people did not like the sparse and crude way that he said it, but still didn't challenge the general validity of it. And do you know why no one challenged it? Because it indeed was a true statement. It was a devil-minded statement that is nevertheless made true only because of the undeniable fact that all of America's mainstream social systems failed black people in the past and still continue to fail black people. And I do mean ALL of them, literally, with no exceptions. The economic system, the judicial system, the education system, federal, state, and local government systems, the political system, the welfare system, the credit system, the voting system, the media systems, the banking system, the housing system, the social security system, our foreign policy system, the labor system, the health care system, the child support system, etc.; each and every one has failed us. And there are three reasons why every systematized organization in America has always failed and will continue to fail black people: either they were not originally designed with black people in mind; they have a measure of racism built into it them; and/or they have a large number of racist people active within them—all of which amounts to the same effect. This is the America that the black race has always known, generation after generation, despite the fact that some people, even some blacks, never want to openly acknowledge that or accept it as reality.

After Trump made that statement, which was made as if to signify to black people that he would do differently than all the past presidents and actively work toward our best interest if elected, he then won the presidency and has subsequently proceeded to do the opposite of what he seemingly promised black people he would do, and then some. Which, if you are "woke," was to be expected. In doing this, Trump is merely following in the footsteps of all those who held that office before him, and setting more of the same evil precedent for those who will hold it after him. Many other politicians have made similar statements and soundbite promises that were directed at black people during their campaigns, and they all did the same thing for black people that Trump has done once they are elected—they put forth no policies that would help black people, but put forth plenty of policies that would hurt black people. I really do not understand why they ever bother to promise black people anything, knowing that they won't keep those promises and that it probably won't even hurt them much during their re-election bids. Barack Obama, ironically, is one of the presidents that never really promised black people much while on the campaign trails, and certainly, once elected, wasn't able to deliver black people much of anything that will be long-lasting and tangible. (I honestly believe that Obama had long known that he really couldn't do much for black people, both because of the stifling inherently racist white supremacist system he had to work within as well as the potential repercussions that could befall him if he suddenly appeared, to the power establishment, to be too strident in such an effort. Like what happened to Abraham Lincoln, John and Robert Kennedy, and Martin Luther King Jr. However, in his political retirement, Obama has spoken out and warned black people about the potential for the reawakening of state-sponsored white supremacy in America.[96]) But the really sad part about this repetitive political scenario is that many black people continue to place their belief and hope in politicians and the social systems they represent and build, and flat out refuse to learn from the lessons of history.

At the end of the day, and at the very least, it's about having a very realistic understanding of the society that we live in and the various social systems that make it work, or not work. A society is defined as "a group of people involved in persistent social interaction and who share the same geographical territory and are typically subject to the same political authorities and dominant cultural expectations."[97] For societies to be able to function in a proper and organized fashion, patterned ways of doing common things have to get firmly established, and these patterns are what we refer to as "social systems." Social systems are "the patterned series of interrelationships existing between individuals, groups, and institutions, forming a coherent whole—the formal organization of status and role that may develop among the members of a society."[98] So while black people have always been an integral part of American society, we've rarely been an integral part of the power circles that create and define America's social systems. And this isn't to suggest that the mere presence of black people within any governmental environment or institution or company always works to the good of the black collective. In my first book, I make the point that since 1964 the number of black elected officials had increased from 103 to well over 8,000, yet the condition of black America had not gotten marginally better by 2007.[99] There are well over 10,000 black elected officials today,[100] yet this still remains true. This is all due to America's social systems having very strong built-in elements of racism and white supremacy within them, sentiments that are not fading vestiges as some would have us believe, and no black elected official or comparably small contingency of black officials has enough power or influence to override that, even if their intent were to do so. History shows this clearly as well.

Social systems are levers of power—extensions of power within societies. Social systems are created to control various societal processes, for a supposed mixed benefit for the state and the people. But when it comes to black people, we are not often included in the "benefit" aspect of how these systems affect "the people." Most times we have found that, if not outright victimized, we are not treated fairly by these systems. The old adage "history is best qualified to reward research" is really befitting here, and history is clear on the answer as to the question of whether or not America's social systems have served black people well. It is a resounding NO. Therefore, as I stated before, I have never understood why so many black people have so much faith in America's systems, all of which were set up largely by white men who expressly had no good will or good intent towards black people. To that point, I also do not understand why so many of us, despite knowing the relevant history and in spite of our continuous collective social condition, celebrate certain American holidays. I have never understood why so many black people in America seem to believe they are somehow capable of force-feeding the majority of white America the worthy notions of racial equality and fairness. It seems as if many black people in America are all too ready to forget and ignore history. And as long as so many black people continue to do this, certain negative aspects of history will continue to repeat themselves, we will continue to be treated as a powerless second or third-class minority, and future black generations are all but guaranteed to suffer from inequality. Which brings me to yet another very relevant old adage that applies here: Those who refuse to learn from the lessons of history are doomed to repeat them.

A social system, like a law, can be no more just than the people who create and enforce it, meaning that if a large portion of the people in a given society are intently racist, the social systems within that society will inherently be racist, irrespective of any politically correct publicly stated intent. A man-made system has two things: an author and an agenda. In America, white men are typically the authors and creators of the agendas within the social systems, and history, again, clearly shows us what tends to happen whenever and wherever black people are subjected to white male oversight and rule. And though you won't find a social system or law that dares to openly declare itself "racist" in today's times within America, unlike in the very recent past, you would still be hard-pressed to find even one that doesn't have a racist history or that hasn't been routinely applied differently when it comes to a black person vs. a white person, or that isn't currently operating in a racist fashion in one way or another. The child support system is no different in this regard, and I think the information in the previous five chapters of this book has clearly shown that. But the whole truth isn't just that the rules of play are always different for black people in America, and in the world for that matter; but also, that there is usually an accompanying undertone of purposeful anti-black intent to go along with the different rules of play, when you look at many of the general negative affects the applied policies of certain systems have on the black community. In other words, it's not always just simply person-to-person racism that's occurring; within some social systems, there exists a purposeful organized general intent to sabotage, destabilize, and stifle the black community.

I am nowhere near alone in these sentiments. Dr. Amos Wilson, a highly respected world famous theoretical psychologist and Pan-Africanist social scholar, now deceased, is but one standout intellectual who also opined about how the systems within a racist mainstream society, once analyzed, almost always prove out to inherently work against the best interests of the minority peoples in that society, due to purposeful design and/or the personal feelings and actions of racist people who have influence within them. In other words, it doesn't matter if you are a black football player in the NFL like Colin Kaepernick, a black kid playing in the park with a toy gun like Tamir Rice, or the first black president named Barack Obama; you can and will still likely be victimized by systematic racism in America because it is so embedded in nearly everything in our society. Yes, *nearly everything*. We have racist holidays. We have multitudes of racist people on our currency. We have a racist national anthem. We have racist monuments all over this country. We have big cities named after racists. All of the Founding Fathers were unabashedly racists. As a nation, we have and always have had starkly racist foreign policies. We have a racist president in the White House right now, the latest in a long line of many, with a team of racist handlers around him who seemingly are doing their best to make things even worse with regards to race relations in America. It is next to impossible to find any aspect of American society that hasn't been touched by racism. It has always been this way, to one degree or another, and is not on the path to changing anytime soon—the rise of Trumpism and the "alt-right," among other things, clearly showcases that. Racism and white supremacy are as American as warm apple pie or Kool-Aid, and are certainly over-represented in each and every one of America's institutional systems, past and present.

    When you look up Dr. Wilson in Wikipedia, his bio states that he "believed that racism was a *structurally* and *institutionally* driven phenomenon derived from the inequities of power relations between groups, and could persist even if and when the more overt expressions of it were no longer present."[101] Dr. Wilson believed that "racism, then, could only be neutralized by transforming society (structurally) and the system(s) of power relations." On these two points, I concur one hundred and ten percent. Moreover, Dr. Wilson once gave a speech where he spoke very eloquently on the specific topic of black love and *how the systematic destruction of black love is always on the table whenever racist social systems have an influence in black life*, even if such effects initially come about as only an unintended circumstance. Basically, he was saying that within a racist power system you can expect all the social systems to naturally have a racist bend to them, but especially those ones that deal closely with black interpersonal relationships and the exposed fault lines of black familial and communal unity. Instead of seeking to help eliminate or minimize any potential damage with their actions, these social systems always tend to agitate and aggravate black familial and communal fault lines, making the situation even more potentially disruptive than it already was. From the big-picture perspective, this is exactly the affect the U.S. child support system is having on the black community. Here is the excerpt from Dr. Wilson's speech that I find so poignant, and relevant to this issue:

"When you want to destroy a community, you destroy the nature of their romantic love. You destroy their ability to love one another in a healthy sort of way. When you think about the problems we have as people and as individuals in loving each other romantically, you must recognize that, in good part, those problems have been set up by a cruel social system. The love that we have for one another is the greatest threat to the people who rule over us, and it is necessary for those people who rule over us, who rule over African peoples the world over, if those people are to stay in power, they must destroy our ability to love in a healthy sort of way. This is why, even if you're concerned with your individual love for your boyfriend or your husband, you cannot separate that love from what is going on in the world politically and socially. Because the nature of that love is defined by political and social circumstances. And if you can't understand why you have problems in your love relations, perhaps a good part of it is because you have not taken time to understand the nature of the political and social situation in which you live. Because you've been made to think that your love is merely the concern of yourself and your partner and not rooted in what's going on in the world."[102]

I believe Dr. Wilson was absolutely correct in his assessment. Which is why I decided to write this book—to help my people more fully "understand the nature of the political and social circumstances in which you live." And when you do gather a full understanding of it, you won't find it so ironic that the U.S. government first created the child support system as an official affirmative action-like equity program designed to assist white women in overcoming certain post marriage financial and social disadvantages they were assumed to suffer from due to their gender (which they fully understood would not majorly damage the cohesiveness of the white community or place too many white men under hostile judicial supervision or detainment), and yet this same system is being used and applied differently and has an altogether different affect when it comes to the black community. This big difference in affect comes about largely due to the vast gaps that exists between white and black males in America when it comes to economics and power, which is all due to racism since racism is responsible for those differences even existing between the two races in America in the first place. Whites in America have never had to contend with slavery, systematic racism, institutional racism, voter suppression, gentrification, workplace discrimination, redistricting, redlining, mass incarceration, and all of the deep-seated psychological remnants thereof. No system, law, or policy in America can be cited as being specifically created or used in order to work against the best interest of the white population, but there has never been a time in America where black people could say the same. So, it should come as no surprise that America's social systems that do work for them, do *not* in fact work for us. They were never intended to work for us. That being the case, the fact that the inherently racist political and court systems do have so much *black-people-given* power and influence over the torn black families of America is indeed a self-assisted travesty.

Although it is generally true that racism in America today is not as bad as it has been in the past, guess what: it is still bad. Very bad. The application of racism is just more modernized—that's really the only difference between those past eras gone by, and today. And the various old and new social systems of America have been very instrumental tools in keeping racism and white supremacy alive and well and effective on a massive scale. We must fully acknowledge and fully take into consideration the fact that the social systems of America, especially the legal system, have *always* saw fit to attribute to black people, especially black males, a "special" kind of status. Thus, blacks have always had to carefully navigate through overt and covert racism and other negative nuances whenever we have to deal with our issues within these systems. Yet, on occasion (whenever they get called out), the curators and proprietors of these very same systems will then attempt to solve the "problems" that they created themselves, thereby confusing skeptics and onlookers as to whether or not there really was some actual purposeful intent on their part in causing the problems in the first place. One somewhat recent example of this sort of thing happened with the passing and enactment of the Federal Mandatory Minimum Sentencing Guidelines and the Crack Cocaine vs. Powder Cocaine Sentencing Laws.[103] These racist laws and policies subsequently led to the over-sentencing and over-incarceration of millions of black males, myself included, since the mid-1980's for possessing extremely small amounts of cocaine in crack form, because research had indicated that crack was mainly sold and possessed by blacks, while possessors of the same amounts of powder cocaine, who were mostly white, were given relative slaps on the wrist. When called out about the racism within these laws many years after they had been in effect, the government subsequently enacted a few changes to those laws and then proclaimed that the obvious targeted effects they'd had on the black populace was never intended and regrettable. But by then, the damage to our communities had already been done. Ten years ago, I was the first person to write a book about it and call them out for it.

With this book, and expressly for the sake and sole benefit of the black community in America, I am calling out the U.S. child support system in that same way, and hope that some positive change can eventually come about as a result. Though having hope isn't a strategy, it can certainly sometimes be a precursor to effective action. With this book, I have shown just how the child support system is currently helping to further separate black families, further destabilize already unstable black communities, fuel the mass incarceration of black males, and effectively poison the potential of future black generations. So, the question that we *collectively* must answer is: Now that we know the facts about how the U.S. child support system affects us, what are we going to do about it?

Notation Sources

1 — https://www.brainyquote.com/quotes/john_stuart_mill_121327
2 — Judge Lynn Toler, quote from *Marriage Boot Camp* T.V. Show, 2017
3 — Hans Sherrer, *99.8% Conviction Rate in U.S. Federal Courts Can Make Japanese Prosecutors Jealous*, JusticeDenied.org, 2016
4 — Devah Pager, Study: Black man and white felon – same chances for hire, ac360.blogs.cnn.com, 2008
5 — Shawn Garrison, *4 Problems with The Modern Child Support System*, DadsDivorce.com, 2017; Julie Garrison, *The Importance of Shared Parenting*, DadsDivorce.com, 2011
6 — Bureau of Justice Statistics
7 — https://www.goodreads.com/author/quotes/2192.Aristotle
8 — http://www.childsupportanalysis.co.uk/information_and_explanation/world/history_usa.htm, Copyright: Barry Pearson, 2003
9 — http://legal-dictionary.thefreedictionary.com/Child+Support
10 — http://www.child-support-laws-state-by-state.com/child-support.html, 2014
11 — Ibid.
12 — Ibid.
13 — https://en.wikipedia.org/wiki/Act_for_the_Relief_of_the_Poor_1601
14 — http://www.child-support-laws-state-by-state.com/child-support.html, 2014; Jennifer Wolf, *The History of Child Support in the U.S.*, TheSpruce.com, 2017; http://www.childsupportanalysis.co.uk/information_and_explanation/world/history_usa.htm, Copyright: Barry Pearson, 2003
15 — http://www.aaregistry.org/historic_events/view/reconstruction-americas-first-attempt-integrate, Copyright: African American Registry, 2000 to 2013
16 — http://www.child-support-laws-state-by-state.com/child-support.html, 2014; Jennifer Wolf, *The History of Child Support in the U.S.*, TheSpruce.com, 2017;

http://www.childsupportanalysis.co.uk/information_and_explanation/world/history_usa.htm, Copyright: Barry Pearson, 2003

17 — Ibid.

18 — Ibid.

19 — Ibid.

20 — Ibid.

21 — Ibid.

22 — Pew Research Center; http://stateofworkingamerica.org/fact-sheets/poverty/, Copyright: Economic Policy Institute

23 — Collier Meyerson, *How Our Racist Child Support Laws Hurt Poor, Black Fathers the Most*, SplinterNews.com, 2016

24 — Supreme Court of The United States, Turner v. Rogers ET AL., 2011 (https://www.supremecourt.gov/opinions/10pdf/10-10.pdf)

25 — Collier Meyerson, *How Our Racist Child Support Laws Hurt Poor, Black Fathers the Most*, SplinterNews.com, 2016

26 — Ibid.

27 — http://www.historynet.com/abraham-lincoln-quotes

28 — Ken Blackwell and Rob Schwarzwalder, *Decline of Black Family on Full Display in Baltimore*, CNSNews.com, 2015; Steve Chapman, *The Black Family in 1965 and Today*, Reason.com, 2015

29 — ChildStats.gov

30 — Kids Count Data Center, Annie E. Casey Foundation, 2017

31 — Jessica Dickerson, *'72 Percent' Documentary Confronts the Black Community's Single-Parent 'Epidemic'*, HuffingtonPost.com, 2014

32 — Pew Research Center, Religion & Public Life

33 — Pew Research Center

34 — Sue Chan, *Broken Homes, Broken Children*, CBSNews.com, 2003

35 — Duff Wilson and John Shiffman, *Newborns Die After Being Sent Home with Mothers Struggling to Kick Drug Addictions*, Reuters.com, 2015

36 — https://www.youtube.com/watch?v=Zm1KEoM2yM0

37 — Matt F., *50 Cent Dragged By His Son Marquise Jackson Over Child Support Joke*, HotNewHipHop.com, 2017

38 — CNN Larry King Live Interview with Judge Judy (http://edition.cnn.com/TRANSCRIPTS/0510/04/lkl.01.html), 2005

39 — Ale Russian, *Tyrese Gibson Sobs "Please Don't Take My Baby" in Emotional Plea to Ex-Wife*, People.com, 2017

40 — U.S. Census Dept.; James Nye, *1 in 3 Children Live Without Their Father as Number of Two-Parent Households Falls by 1.2m in Ten Years*, DailyMail.com, 2012

41 — https://en.wikipedia.org/wiki/First-wave_feminism

42 — https://en.wikipedia.org/wiki/Me_Too_(hashtag)

43 — Collier Meyerson, *How Our Racist Child Support Laws Hurt Poor, Black Fathers the Most*, SplinterNews.com, 2016; Joseph E. Cordell, *3 Ways the Child Support System Rips Apart Families*, HuffingtonPost.com, 2017

44 — National Parents Organization, 2014 Shared Parenting Report Card

45 — Shawn Garrison, *4 Problems with The Modern Child Support System*, DadsDivorce.com, 2017; https://www.youtube.com/watch?v=k9BKXQ8ROlw

46 — Ibid.

47 — http://www.childsupportanalysis.co.uk/information_and_explanation/world/history_usa.htm, Copyright: Barry Pearson, 2003

48 — National Parents Organization, 2014 Shared Parenting Report Card

49 — Dr. L F Lowenstein, *Parental Alienation and the Judiciary*, ParentalAlienationSupport.com, 2012

50 — U.S. Bureau of Labor Statistics; MacroTrends.net

51 — Collier Meyerson, *How Our Racist Child Support Laws Hurt Poor, Black Fathers the Most*, SplinterNews.com, 2016; National Conference of State Legislatures, Criminal Nonsupport and Child Support

52 — Daniel Clement, Esq., *Custodial Parents Interfering with Visitation Lose Custody and Held in Contempt*, ClementLaw.com, 2006

53 — Bobbie Edsor, *12 High-Profile Billionaires and Millionaires Who Aren't Leaving Their Fortunes to Their Children*, BusinessInsider.com, 2017

54 — Song "Welcome to My Hood" by DJ Khalid ft. Rick Ross, Plies, Lil Wayne, & T-Pain (https://genius.com/Dj-khaled-welcome-to-my-hood-lyrics)

55 — Gerald D. Jaynes, *Debt Slavery*, Encyclopaedia Britannica, Inc., 2015; Douglas A. Blackmon, *Slavery by Another Name: The Re-Enslavement of Black Americans From the Civil War to World War II*, Anchor Books, 2008

56 — Peter Baker, *Bill Clinton Concedes His Crime Law Jailed Too Many for Too Long*, The New York Times, 2015; Allison Graves, *Did Hillary Clinton Call African-American Youth 'Superpredators?'*, PolitiFact.com, 2016; Washington Free Beacon Staff, *Haitians Protest Outside Hillary Clinton's Office Over 'Billions Stolen' by Clinton Foundation*, Freebeacon.com, 2015

57 — Bill Quigley, *40 Reasons Our Jails and Prisons Are Full of Black and Poor People*, CommonDreams.org, 2015

58 — Bureau of Justice Statistics

59 — Ibid.

60 — Ibid.

61 — Ibid.

62 — Janice Williams, *Serving Time: Average Prison Sentence in The U.S. is Getting Even Longer*, Newsweek, 2017

63 — Bureau of Justice Statistics

64 — Joseph E. Cordell, *3 Ways the Child Support System Rips Apart Families*, HuffingtonPost.com, 2015

65 — *Poverty Rate by Race/Ethnicity*, KFF.org, 2016

66 — U.S. Current Population Survey and the National Committee on Pay Equity; Bureau of Labor Statistics: Weekly and Hourly Earnings Data from the Current Population Survey

67 — Igor Volsky, *Paul Ryan Blames Poverty on Lazy 'Inner City' Men*, ThinkProgress.org, 2014

68 — Daniel Cadet, *5 Lies We Should Stop Telling About Black Fatherhood*, HuffingtonPost.com, 2014; Shawn Garrison, *New Study Debunks Deadbeat Dad Myth*, DadsDivorce.com, 2015

69 — Joseph E. Cordell, *3 Ways the Child Support System Rips Apart Families*, HuffingtonPost.com, 2015; *African-American Men Suffer After Divorce, Study Finds* (https://news.unt.edu/news-releases/african-american-men-suffer-after-divorce-study-finds), University of North Texas, 1999

70 — U.S. General Accounting Office Report; Julie Garrison, *Child Support Case Study: Jailing Dads Who Can't Pay*, MensRights.com/Cordell & Cordell Domestic Litigation Firm, 2016

71 — Collier Meyerson, *How Our Racist Child Support Laws Hurt Poor, Black Fathers the Most*, SplinterNews.com, 2016

72 — Ibid.

73 — Ibid.

74 — US Department of Health and Human Services

75 — Angela Bronner Helm, *Black Women Now the Most Educated Group in U.S.*, TheRoot.com, 2016; Joseph E. Cordell, *3 Ways the Child Support System Rips Apart Families*, HuffingtonPost.com, 2015

76 — National Conference of State Legislatures, Interest on Child Support Arrears

77 — Bureau of Labor Statistics

78 — Linda Holmes, *ESPN's 'Broke' Looks At the Many Ways Athletes Lose Their Money*, Npr.org, 2012

79 — Tom Feran, *Settlement Reached in Lawsuit on Singer Sean Levert's Death in Cuyahoga County Jail*, blog.cleveland.com, 2010

80 — Omar Burgess, *Juvenile Reportedly Jailed Over Owing $150,000 in Child Support*, Complex.com, 2017

81 — Corey Sipkin, *Former Boxing Champ Zab Judah Jailed for Being a Deadbeat Dad*, New York Daily News, 2017

82 — TJB Writer, *Mike Epps Officially Divorced, Paying Ex 25k in Spousal Support + 15k For Kids*, TheJasmineBrand.com, 2017

83 — The Federal Reserve Board

84 — Tennessee Department of Human Services

85 — City-Data.com, Memphis

86 — Ibid.

87 — Ibid.

88 — Cameron Huddleston, *More Than Half of Americans Have Less Than $1,000 in Savings in 2017*, GoBankingRates.com, 2017

89 — J.B. Wogan, *Trump Leaves Obama's Last Minute Child Support Rule Alone*, Governing.com, 2017

90 — Bureau of Justice Statistics

91 — J.B. Wogan, *Trump Leaves Obama's Last Minute Child Support Rule Alone*, Governing.com, 2017

92 — Lauren Victoria, *Is Trump Right? A Look at What Obama's Done for Black Community*, NBCNews.com, 2015

93 — Bureau of Labor Statistics

94 — Ibid.

95 — Tom LoBianco and Ashley Killough, *Trump Pitches Black Voters: 'What the Hell Do You Have to Lose?'*, CNN.com, 2016

96 — Jennifer Smith, *Barack Obama Appears to Compare Trump Presidency to the Rise of Hitler and Says US Democracy Could 'Fall Apart Very Quickly'*, DailyMail.com, 2017

97 — https://en.wikipedia.org/wiki/Society

98 — https://en.wikipedia.org/wiki/Social_system

99 — National Urban League

100 — Ibid.

101 — https://en.wikipedia.org/wiki/Amos_N._Wilson

102 — https://www.youtube.com/watch?v=6wRt1BatksU

103 — FAMM, *Crack Cocaine Mandatory Minimum Sentences* (http://famm.org/projects/federal/us-congress/crack-cocaine-mandatory-minimum-sentences/)

CPSIA information can be obtained
at www.ICGtesting.com
Printed in the USA
BVHW041632250221
600902BV00011B/733

9 780979 295362